Oxford AQA GCSE History

Britain: Migration, Empires and the People c790-Present Day

Revision Guide

- RECAP
- APPLY
- REVIEW
- SUCCEED

Changes to the AQA GCSE History specification 8145 (Version 1.3) and support for these changes

AQA released Version 1.3 of their AQA GCSE History specification in September 2019. The changes are to the command words and stems to a number of the AQA GCSE History questions to make the demands of the questions clearer for all students. Please refer to the AQA website for more information.

To support you with these changes, this book has been written to match the updated specification.

Aaron Wilkes   Lindsay Bruce

OXFORD UNIVERSITY PRESS

OXFORD
UNIVERSITY PRESS

Great Clarendon Street, Oxford, OX2 6DP, United Kingdom

Oxford University Press is a department of the University of Oxford.

It furthers the University's objective of excellence in research, scholarship, and education by publishing worldwide. Oxford is a registered trade mark of Oxford University Press in the UK and in certain other countries.

© Oxford University Press 2021

The moral rights of the authors have been asserted.

First published in 2021

All rights reserved. No part of this publication may be reproduced, stored in a retrieval system, or transmitted, in any form or by any means, without the prior permission in writing of Oxford University Press, or as expressly permitted by law, by licence or under terms agreed with the appropriate reprographics rights organization. Enquiries concerning reproduction outside the scope of the above should be sent to the Rights Department, Oxford University Press, at the address above.

You must not circulate this work in any other form and you must impose this same condition on any acquirer.

British Library Cataloguing in Publication Data

Data available

978-1-38-201503-5

Digital edition 978-1-38-201504-2

5 7 9 10 8 6 4

Paper used in the production of this book is a natural, recyclable product made from wood grown in sustainable forests.

The manufacturing process conforms to the environmental regulations of the country of origin.

Printed in Great Britain by Bell and Bain Ltd. Glasgow.

Acknowledgements

The publisher would like to thank Jon Cloake for his work on the Student Book on which this Revision Guide is based and David Rawlings for reviewing this Revision Guide. The publisher would also like to thank Christopher Edge for offering his contribution in the development of this book.

The publishers would like to thank the following for permissions to use their photographs:

Cover: FPG/Staff/Getty Images

p11: VectorShop / Shutterstock.p13: Heritage Images/Contributor/Getty Images;
p22: Mary Evans Picture Library; **p29**: Mary Evans/Library of Congress; **p31**: The Print Collector/Alamy Stock Photo; **p35**: Walker Art Library / Alamy Stock Photo;
p41: Pictorial Press Ltd/Alamy Stock Photo;
p53: Associated Newspapers Ltd./Solo Syndication; **p55**: Charles Hewitt/Getty Images; p56l: VectorShop/Shutterstock; **p56r**: Loveshop/Shutterstock;
p57: John Stoddart/Popperfoto/Contributor/Getty Images; **p60**: Chronicle/Alamy Stock Photo.

Artworks: Aptara, Moreno Chiacchiera, Rudolf Farkas, Martin Sanders, and QBS Learning.

Although we have made every effort to trace and contact all copyright holders before publication this has not been possible in all cases. If notified, the publisher will rectify any errors or omissions at the earliest opportunity.

Links to third party websites are provided by Oxford in good faith and for information only. Oxford disclaims any responsibility for the materials contained in any third party website referenced in this work.

From the author, Lindsay Bruce: to my wonderful husband who did every bedtime and park trip so I could write this. Without you I couldn't do it.
For Jean who I hope is impressed by all of this one day. Finally, everyone at OUP - you are a wonderful bunch. Thank you for your continued support!

From the author: Aaron Wilkes wishes to acknowledge the hard work and practical advice of Emma Jones, Becky Breuer, Melanie Waldron, Harriet Power and Alison Schrecker.

Contents

Introduction to this Revision Guide 5

Top revision tips 6

Master your exam skills 7

How to master the source question 7

How to master the 'significance' question 8

How to master the 'similarity/difference' question 8

How to master the 'main factors' question 9

AQA GCSE History mark schemes 10

Britain: Migration, Empires and the People c790–Present Day Timeline 11

Part one:
Conquered and conquerors

1 Invasion 12

Anglo-Saxon and Viking invasion of Britain 12

Cnut, Emma and the North Sea Empire 14

2 A Norman Kingdom and 'Angevin' Empire 16

England and the Norman Empire 16

The 'Angevin' Empire 18

3 The birth of English identity 20

The Hundred Years War 20

Part two:
Looking west

4 Sugar and the Caribbean 22

Tudor and Stuart explorers look west 22

The move to slavery 24

5 Colonisation in North America 26

British colonies in America 26

The British lose their American colonies 28

6 Migrants to and from Britain 30

Huguenot migration, Ulster Plantations and Highland Clearances 30

Contents

RECAP **APPLY** **REVIEW**

Part three: Expansion and empire

7 Expansion in India — 32

- British control in India — 32
- Indian discontent — 34
- Impact of Empire on Britain and India — 36

8 Expansion in Africa — 38

- The scramble for Africa — 38
- Expansion continues — 40
- The Boer War of 1899–1902 — 42

9 Migrants to, from and within Britain — 44

- Irish and Jewish migration to Britain — 44
- People on the move in nineteenth-century Britain — 46

Part four: Britain in the twentieth century

10 The end of the British Empire — 48

- Reasons for the end of the British Empire — 48
- The Suez Crisis, 1956 — 50

11 The legacy of the British Empire — 52

- Immigration to Britain after the Second World War — 52
- The Commonwealth — 54
- The Falklands War, 1982 — 56

12 Britain's relationship with Europe — 58

- Britain and Europe — 58

Exam practice: GCSE sample answers — 60

Activity answers guidance — 66

Glossary — 70

Introduction

The *Oxford AQA GCSE History* textbook series has been developed by an expert team led by Jon Cloake and Aaron Wilkes. This matching revision guide offers you step-by-step strategies to master your AQA Thematic Study: Migration, empires and the people exam skills, and the structured revision approach of **Recap, Apply and Review** to prepare you for exam success.

Use the **Progress checklists** on pages 3–4 to keep track of your revision, and use the traffic light ☹☺☻ feature on each page to monitor your confidence level on each topic. Other exam practice and revision features include **Top revision tips** on page 6, and the **'How to...'** guides for each exam question type on pages 7–9.

RECAP
Each chapter recaps key events and developments through easy-to-digest chunks and visual diagrams. **Key terms** appear in bold and red font; they are defined in the glossary. (SB) indicates the relevant Oxford AQA History Student Book pages so you could easily re-read the textbook for further revision.

SUMMARY highlights the most important facts at the end of each chapter.

TIMELINE provides a short list of dates to help you remember key events.

APPLY
Each revision activity is designed to help drill your understanding of facts, and then progress towards applying your knowledge to exam questions.

These targeted revision activities are written specifically for this guide, which will help you apply your knowledge towards the four exam questions in your AQA Migration, empires and the people exam paper:

SOURCE ANALYSIS   **EXPLAIN THE SIGNIFICANCE**   **SIMILARITY/DIFFERENCE**   **FACTORS**

- **Examiner Tip** highlights key parts of an exam question, and gives you hints on how to avoid common mistakes in exams.
- **Revision Skills** provides different revision techniques. Research shows that using a variety of revision styles can help cement your revision.
- **Review** gives you helpful reminders about how to check your answers and how to revise further.

REVIEW
Throughout each chapter, you can review and reflect on the work you have done, and find advice on how to further refresh your knowledge.

You can tick off the Review column from the Progress checklists as you work through this revision guide. **Activity answers guidance** and the **Exam practice** sections with full sample student answers also help you to review your own work.

Top revision tips

Getting your revision right

It is perfectly natural to feel anxious when exam time approaches. The best way to keep on top of the stress is to be organised!

3 months to go

Plan: create a realistic revision timetable, and stick to it!
Track your progress: use the Progress checklists (pages 3–4) to help you track your revision. It will help you stick to your revision plan.
Be realistic: revise in regular, small chunks, of around 30 minutes. Reward yourself with 10 minute breaks – you will be amazed how much more you'll remember.
Positive thinking: motivate yourself by turning your negative thoughts to positive ones. Instead of asking *'why can't I remember this topic at all?'* ask yourself *'what different techniques can I try to improve my memory?'*
Organise: make sure you have everything you need – your revision books, coloured pens, index cards, sticky notes, paper, etc. Find a quiet place where you are comfortable. Divide your notes into sections that are easy to use.
Timeline: create a timeline with colour-coded sticky notes, to make sure you remember important dates relating to the three parts of the Migration, empires and the people thematic study (use the Timeline on page 11 as a starting point).
Practise: ask your teachers for practise questions or past papers.

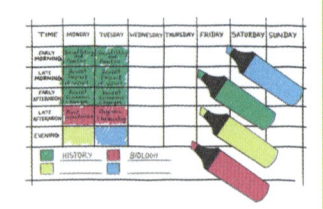

Revision techniques

Using a variety of revision techniques can help you remember information, so try out different methods:

- Make **flashcards**, using both sides of the card to test yourself on key figures, dates, and definitions
- **Colour-code** your notebooks
- **Reread** your textbook or copy out your notes
- Create **mind-maps** for complicated topics
- Draw **pictures** and symbols that spring to mind
- Group study
- Find a **buddy** or group to revise with and test you
- Listen to revision **podcasts** or watch revision **clips**
- Work through the **revision activities** in this guide.

Revision tips to help you pass your Migration, empires and the people exam

1 month to go

Big picture: make sure you are familiar with examples – from the different periods you have studied – of the factors relating to this Thematic Study: war; religion; government; economic resources; science and technology; ideas such as imperialism, social Darwinism and civilisation; and the role of individuals.
Identify your weaknesses: which topics or question types are easier and which are more challenging for you? Schedule more time to revise the challenging topics or question types.
Make it stick: find memorable ways to remember chronology, using fun rhymes, or doodles, for example.
Take a break: do something completely different during breaks – listen to music, take a short walk, make a cup of tea, for example.
Check your answers: answer the exam questions in this guide, then check the Activity answers guidance at the end of the guide to practise applying your knowledge to exam questions.
Understand your mark scheme: review the Mark scheme (page 10) for each exam question, and make sure you understand how you will be marked.
Master your exam skills: study and remember the How to master your exam skills steps (pages 7–9) for each AQA question type – it will help you plan your answers quickly!
Time yourself: practise making plans and answering exam questions within the recommended time limits.
Take mock exams seriously: you can learn from them how to manage your time better under exam conditions.
Rest well: make sure your phone and laptop are put away at least an hour before bed. This will help you rest better.

On the big day

Sleep early: Don't work through the night, get a good night's sleep.
Be prepared: Make sure you know where and when the exam is, and leave plenty of time to get there.
Check: make sure you have all your equipment in advance, including spare pens!
Drink and eat healthily: avoid too much caffeine or junk food. Water is best – if you are 5% dehydrated, then your concentration drops 20%.
Stay focused: don't listen to people who might try to wind you up about what might come up in the exam – they don't know any more than you.
Good luck!

Master your exam skills

Get to grips with your Paper 2: Migration, Empires and the People Thematic Study

The Paper 2 exam lasts 2 hours, and you must answer eight questions covering two topics. The first four questions (worth 44 marks) will cover the Thematic Study; the last four questions (40 marks) will cover your British Depth Study topic. Here, you will find details about what to expect from the first four questions which relate to the Migration, empires and the people Thematic Study, and advice on how to master your exam skills.

You should spend about 50 minutes in total on the Migration, Empires and the People questions – see pages 8–9 for how long to spend on each question. The four questions will always follow this pattern:

▼ SOURCE A

01 Study **Source A**. How useful is **Source A** to a historian studying …? Explain your answer using **Source A** and your contextual knowledge. [8 marks]

02 Explain the significance of … [8 marks]

03 Explain **two ways** in which… were similar/different. [8 marks]

04 Has … been the main factor in …? Explain your answer with reference to … and other factors. [16 marks] [SPaG 4 marks]

REVIEW

If you find FACTORS challenging, look out for the FACTORS activities throughout this guide to help you revise and drill your understanding of the FACTORS questions. Look out for the REVISION SKILLS tips too, to inspire you to find the revision strategies that work for you!

How to master the source question

This question targets your understanding of how useful the source is to a historian. Usually, the source will be an image (a cartoon or drawing, for example), but in some years a textual source may be used. Here are the steps to consider when answering the source question.

Question 1

- **Content:** Look at the source carefully. What point is the artist or writer making about the subject? Circle or underline any key points or arguments that are made.
- **Provenance**: Consider the time in which the source was created. What topic or event does the source relate to? Use the provenance (caption) of the source to think about where the source was created, the circumstances of the creator, how much information they had, and their purpose and audience.
- **Context:** Now think back over your own knowledge. Write about whether the content and caption fit with what you know. Does it give a fair reflection of the person, event or issue it describes?

REVISION SKILLS

Read the *British Depth Study Revision Guide* for help on the last 4 questions of Paper 2.

EXAMINER TIP

Remember that this question is similar to the source question in Paper 1, but this focuses on just *one* source.

EXAMINER TIP

This question requires you to think about the significance of something. You have to consider the contemporary, short- and long-term impact of an event or development.

EXAMINER TIP

This question is worth a lot of marks and requires a longer answer. Make sure you leave plenty of time to complete it at the end of the exam. Don't forget that you get up to 4 marks for spelling, punctuation and grammar (SPaG) on this question too.

Master your exam skills

- **Comment:** You need to make a judgement about how useful the source is. A good way to work towards an answer is to think about what is 'inside' the source (that may be the image or text) and what is 'outside' the source (the provenance). These two pieces of information affect the usefulness of a source for a historian studying a particular topic.
- ⏱ Spend about 10 minutes answering this 8-mark question.

EXAMINER TIP

Don't forget that every source is useful for something. Don't start telling the examiner what you *can't* use the source for; no source will tell you everything, so just focus on what it *does* say.

How to master the 'significance' question

Judging the significance of a person or event is about looking at the impact that the person/event had *at the time*, how it affected people *in the long term*, and whether it is still relevant *today*. Here are the steps to consider for answering the 'significance' question.

Question 2

- **Plan:** Consider the immediate importance or impact (short term) of a person/event and their importance later on (long term). Look at the diagram carefully to help you plan:

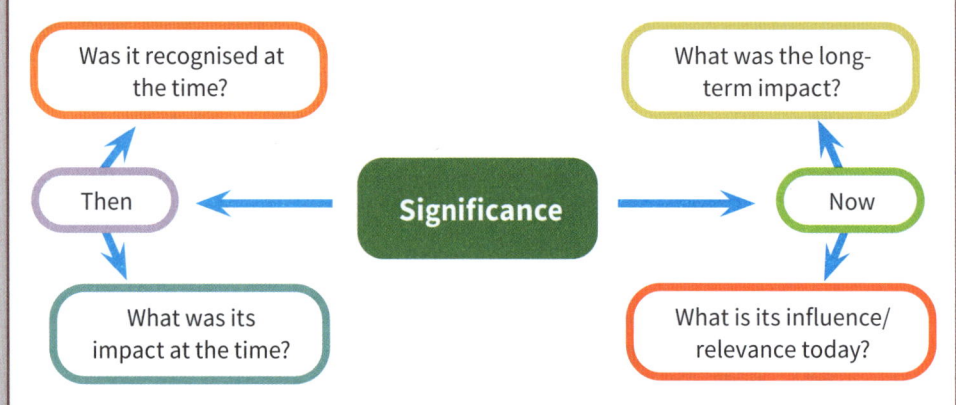

Significance diagram:
- Was it recognised at the time?
- What was the long-term impact?
- Then
- Now
- What was its impact at the time?
- What is its influence/relevance today?

- **Explain the significance:** You need to say what *impact* the person/event made, and whether it had an impact at the time and/or now. In what ways did it have an impact on the wider historical period? Did it affect people's lives? Did it have an impact on politics or the government? Did it lead to change? What happened as a result of it?
- ⏱ Spend about 10 minutes answering this 8-mark question.

EXAMINER TIP

You should also be aware that the significance of an event may change over time. Some things might not be seen as important at the time, but years later, they can be identified as having had a key impact. Or vice versa!

EXAMINER TIP

You should aim to consider at least two aspects of the significance of the person/event. The key with significance is that the person/event will have had an impact at the time *and* will still be seen to have an impact later on in order to be a 'significant' person/event.

How to master the 'similarity/difference' question

Here are the steps to consider for answering the 'similarity/difference' question. This question asks you to consider the similarities or differences between two events or developments.

Question 3

- **Plan:** Make a list or a mind-map to help you analyse the similarities or differences between the two events/developments. What historical facts do you know about the similarities or differences for each of the event/development?
- **Write:** When you have chosen two similarities or differences you want to write about, organise them into two paragraphs, one for each. Consider these points for each paragraph:
    - **Causes:** think about the ways in which the two events have similar or different causes.

EXAMINER TIP

Remember you only have about 1 minute to plan. Examiners are looking for at least 2 similarities or 2 differences that you can explain in detail, so circle 2 similarities or differences you wrote down that you are most confident about.

Master your exam skills

- **Development:** consider what you know about what happened in both events. Look for points of similarity or difference that you can identify and explain.
- **Consequences:** think about the results of the events — again identify and explain similarities or differences.
- ⏱ Spend about 10 minutes answering this 8-mark question.

How to master the 'main factors' question

The last question on Migration, empires and the people in Paper 2 is a question on 'main factors'. It carries the highest mark, along with 4 marks for spelling, punctuation and grammar. The question gives you the opportunity to 'show off' your knowledge of the whole Migration, empires and the people Thematic Study and select information that shows the influence of factors in history, such as religion, war, chance, government, communication, science and technology, and the role of the individual.

Question 4

- **Read the question carefully:** The question will name one factor. Circle the named factor. What topic is the question asking you to consider? The topic is located at the end of the first sentence. Underline the topic to help you focus your answer.
- **Plan your essay:** You could plan your essay by listing the named factor and other factors that caused the event/issue stated in the question:

Named factor 1	Another factor 2	Another factor 3

Write in anything you could use as evidence for the different factors, but make sure that your answer is relevant to the topic of the Thematic Study that has been asked in the question (the one you underlined).

- **Write your essay:** Aim for about four paragraphs. First, write about the influence of the named factor in relation to the topic asked in the question. Write a paragraph each about two more factors in addition to the one named in the question. Lastly, you will have to come to a judgement (a clear conclusion) about whether you agree that the named factor was the main factor. Try to weigh up the named factor against the other ones you wrote about, and say which was more important.
- **Check your SPaG:** Don't forget that you get up to 4 marks for your SPaG in this answer. It's a good idea to leave time to check your SPaG.
- ⏱ This question is worth 16 marks plus 4 SPaG marks. Spend around 20 minutes on it, but this needs to include time to plan and to check your SPaG.

EXAMINER TIP

Don't forget you will have to answer 4 more questions, relating to your British Depth Study topic, in Paper 2. Ensure you leave enough time to complete both sections of Paper 2! You are advised to spend 50 minutes on your British Depth Study.

EXAMINER TIP

Remember that you only have about 2–3 minutes to plan and 15–17 minutes to write your paragraphs. For each factor, choose two historical facts from the history of Migration, empires and the people you are most confident about, and highlight these.

EXAMINER TIP

To back up your conclusion, you should explain *why* you came to that judgement, with supporting evidence. Answers that demonstrate a broad knowledge of examples from across the whole Thematic Study are more likely to gain higher marks.

REVIEW

You can find sample student answers to each Migration, empires and the people question type in the Exam practice pages at the end of this Revision Guide.

AQA GCSE History mark schemes

Below are simplified versions of the AQA mark schemes, to help you understand the marking criteria for your **Paper 2 Britain: Migration, Empires and the People Thematic Study** exam.

Level	Question 1 Source question
4	• Complex evaluation of the source • Argument is shown throughout the answer about how useful the source is, supported by evidence from provenance *and* content, and relevant facts [7–8 marks]
3	• Developed evaluation of the source • Argument is stated about how useful the source is, supported by evidence from source content and/or provenance [5–6 marks]
2	• Simple evaluation of source • Answer is shown about how useful the source is, based on content and/or provenance [3–4 marks]
1	• Basic analysis on the source • Basic description of the source is shown [1–2 marks]

Level	Question 2 Significance question
4	• Complex explanation of aspects of significance • A range of accurate, detailed and relevant facts are shown [7–8 marks]
3	• Developed explanation of aspects of significance • A range of accurate, relevant facts are shown [5–6 marks]
2	• Simple explanation of one aspect of significance • Specific relevant facts are shown [3–4 marks]
1	• Basic explanation of aspect(s) of significance • Some basic related facts are shown [1–2 marks]

Level	Question 3 Similarity/difference question
4	• Complex explanation of similarities or differences • A range of accurate, detailed and relevant facts are shown [7–8 marks]
3	• Developed explanation of similarities or differences • A range of accurate, relevant facts are shown [5–6 marks]
2	• Simple explanation of one similarity or difference • Specific relevant facts are shown [3–4 marks]
1	• Basic explanation of similarity or difference • Some basic related facts are shown [1–2 marks]

Level	Question 4 Main factors question
4	• Complex explanation of named factor *and* other factor(s) • Argument is shown throughout the structured answer, supported by a range of accurate, detailed and relevant facts [13–16 marks]
3	• Developed explanation of the named factor *and* other factor(s) • Argument is shown throughout the structured answer, supported by a range of accurate and relevant facts [9–12 marks]
2	• Simple explanation of the stated factor or other factor(s) • Argument is shown, supported by relevant facts [5–8 marks]
1	• Basic explanation of one or more factors • Some basic facts are shown [1–4 marks]

You also achieve up to 4 marks for spelling, punctuation and grammar (SPaG) on the main factors question:

Level	Question 4 Main factors question SPaG marks
Excellent	• SPaG is accurate throughout the answer • Meaning is very clear • A *wide* range of key historical terms are used accurately [4 marks]
Good	• SPaG shown with considerable accuracy • Meaning is generally clear • A range of key historical terms are used [2–3 marks]
Satisfactory	• SPaG shown with some accuracy • SPaG allows historical understanding to be shown • Basic historical terms are used [1 marks]

Britain: Migration, Empires and the People c790–Present Day Timeline

The symbols represent different types of event as follows:

🌍 migration   ⚔ war   📜 political   🇬🇧 empire

878 ⚔ Vikings control eastern and north-eastern area of Britain (known as the Danelaw)

1066 ⚔ The Normans from France defeat Anglo-Saxon King Harold at the Battle of Hastings

1337–1453 ⚔ The Hundred Years War between England and France

1562 🇬🇧 John Hawkins transports enslaved people to Spanish colonies, starting British involvement in the slave trade

1607 🇬🇧 First successful English settlement (Jamestown) on mainland of North America. British colonisation in North America involves the seizure of territory from indigenous American tribes

1670 🌍 Huguenot (Protestant) settlers begin to arrive in Britain from France in large numbers

1757 ⚔ British victory at the Battle of Plassey allows East India Company to take over Bengal, one of the richest parts of India

1775–82 ⚔ Britain's defeat in the War of Independence results in the loss of the American colonies

1780 🌍 Highland Clearances begin in Scotland

1845–49 🌍 Irish potato famine sees mass starvation in Ireland and the emigration of around one million people

1857–58 ⚔ Indian Rebellion results in India coming under the formal control of the British government

1881–1914 🇬🇧 Scramble for Africa sees the invasion and colonisation of most of Africa by Britain and other European powers

1899–1902 ⚔ The Second Boer War is fought between Dutch settlers (the Boers) and the British army

1947 🇬🇧 India gains independence from Britain

1948 🌍 *Empire Windrush* arrives in Britain, beginning a new period of West Indian migration

1973 📜 Britain joins the European Union

1982 ⚔ The Falklands War between Britain and Argentina over the disputed Falkland Islands near South America takes place

1999 📜 Twelve members of the EU adopt the Euro as their currency, but Britain continues to use the Pound

CHAPTER 1 Invasion

RECAP

Anglo-Saxon and Viking invasion of Britain

For thousands of years different groups of people have been moving to Britain and settling for various reasons. Although Britain is well known for having had a large **empire**, there have been times when Britain was part of another country's empire.

The Anglo-Saxons

From around AD400 onwards, **tribes** from modern-day Denmark and northern Germany (called Angles, Saxons and Jutes) invaded, and later settled in Britain. Collectively they were known as Anglo-Saxons. They set up a number of different kingdoms, led by lords and chieftains — by AD800 some had become very wealthy. By AD800 most Anglo-Saxons had converted to Christianity.

The Vikings

- The **Vikings** were from Scandinavia and began raiding Britain around the AD790s.
- Initially, they raided monasteries (Lindisfarne in Northumbria, for example) and villages near the coast.
- Later they sailed up rivers and attacked further inland, even setting up camps.

Why did the Vikings invade Britain?

- They knew how wealthy some of the Anglo-Saxon kingdoms had become
- Better farming land — Norway was very hilly and Denmark had sandy soil
- Opportunities for younger brothers who did not inherit land in Scandinavia
- Scandinavia was becoming overcrowded

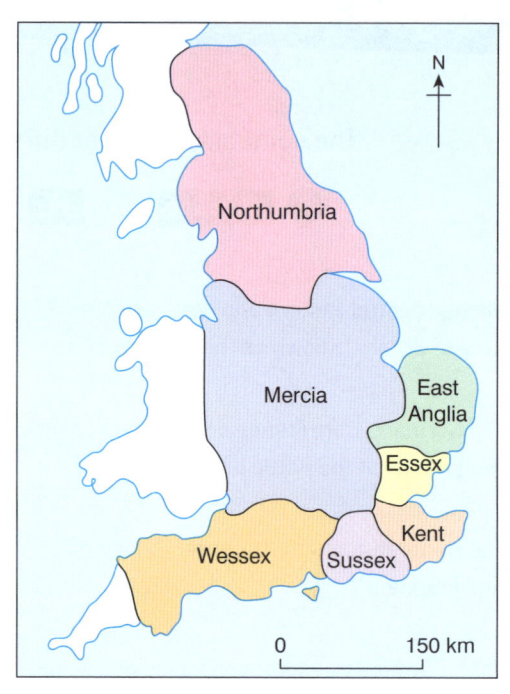

▲ Anglo-Saxon kingdoms around AD700

Wessex and Danelaw

In AD871, Alfred, the 22-year-old son of Aethelred of Wessex, became king after his father's death. He would go on to be known as Alfred the Great and become king of the Anglo-Saxons. He fought the Vikings and helped to bring peace to the country

In AD876, after conquering Northumbria, East Anglia and most of Mercia, the Vikings now turned their attention to Wessex and began a series of attacks

After some early successes, King Alfred and his army were driven back and forced to hide on the Isle of Athelney in the Somerset marshes

In May AD878, King Alfred beat the Vikings at the Battle of Edington in Wiltshire, and the two sides sat down to agree peace terms

The Viking leader, Guthrum, had to become a Christian and agree never to attack Wessex again

A boundary was created between the Anglo-Saxon and Viking territories. The Vikings were to live in the north and east of the country which was called the **Danelaw**

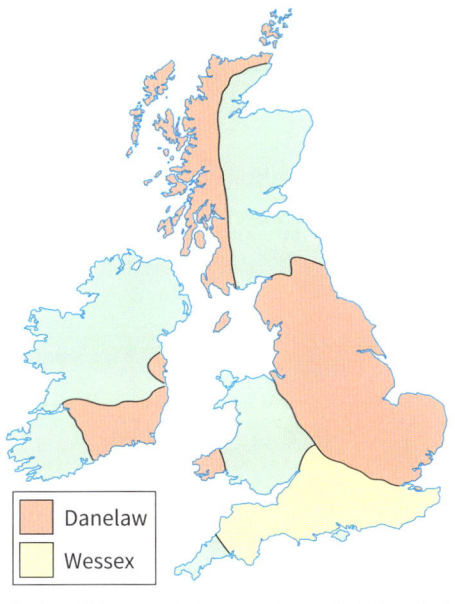

A lasting peace?

- During Alfred's reign (AD871–899), there were still Viking raids on Anglo-Saxon territory.
- However, Alfred strengthened defences across the country to make his land more secure.
- Many Vikings in the Danelaw settled down and lived fairly peacefully with the Anglo-Saxons.
- People travelled and traded between Wessex and the Danelaw, and there was intermarriage between Vikings and Anglo-Saxons.
- Other kingdoms in England acknowledged Alfred to be the 'overlord' and under his rule the Anglo-Saxons began to call themselves Angelcynn (English).
- After Alfred's death, his descendants managed to recapture parts of the Danelaw. However, the Viking presence and influence still remained.
- By the time Alfred's great-grandson (Edgar the peaceful) became king in AD959, the country was settled as it had been for generations.

▲ *The division of Britain at the end of the ninth century. Danelaw, where the Vikings conquered and settled, and Alfred's kingdom of Wessex*

APPLY

SOURCE ANALYSIS

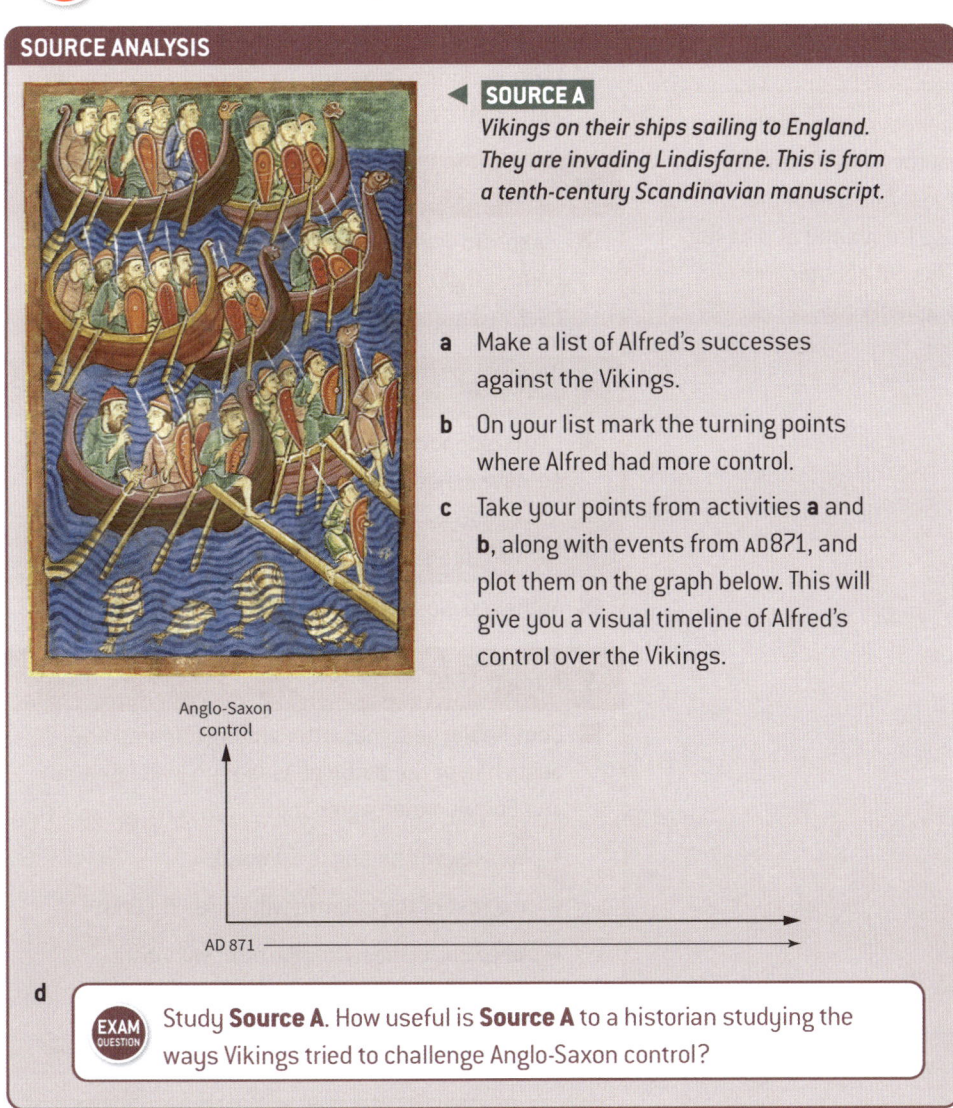

SOURCE A
Vikings on their ships sailing to England. They are invading Lindisfarne. This is from a tenth-century Scandinavian manuscript.

a Make a list of Alfred's successes against the Vikings.

b On your list mark the turning points where Alfred had more control.

c Take your points from activities **a** and **b**, along with events from AD871, and plot them on the graph below. This will give you a visual timeline of Alfred's control over the Vikings.

d Study **Source A**. How useful is **Source A** to a historian studying the ways Vikings tried to challenge Anglo-Saxon control?

REVISION SKILLS

Create a fact test with 10 questions to test detailed knowledge about a topic – this will help you remember new names and dates. You can swap the test with a friend.

EXAMINER TIP

Try to link something you can see in the picture with the provenance and your own knowledge/answers from activities **a** and **b**.

Britain: Migration, Empires and the People c790–Present Day

RECAP

Cnut, Emma and the North Sea Empire

In the tenth century the English re-conquered much of the land held by the Vikings. Under King Edgar the Peaceful, the country became both calm and stable; but when he died in 975, things began to unravel.

In 978 Aethelred became king after his supporters murdered his half-brother Edward. Aethelred was considered a poor judge of character and was taken advantage of by his advisers.

King Aethelred's reign, 978–1013

In 991, a huge Viking army, led by the Dane Sven Forkbeard and the Norwegian Olaf Tryggvason, arrived at Folkestone in a fleet of over 90 ships

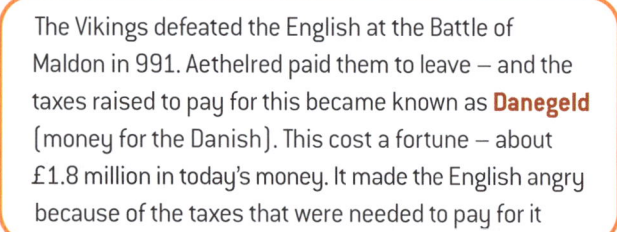

The Vikings defeated the English at the Battle of Maldon in 991. Aethelred paid them to leave – and the taxes raised to pay for this became known as **Danegeld** (money for the Danish). This cost a fortune – about £1.8 million in today's money. It made the English angry because of the taxes that were needed to pay for it

To stop paying Danegeld, Aethelred made a deal with the Normans which stated that they would support each other against their enemies. This meant the Vikings would not be able to use Normandy as a base to launch attacks on Britain. This did not stop the Vikings from attempting to conquer Britain

Edmund and Cnut, 1014–35

Timeline

▼ **November 1002**
- Aethelred carries out a mass killing of all Viking men, women and children that he can find south of the Danelaw. This becomes known as the St Brice's Day Massacre

▼ **1013**
- Sven Forkbeard, the King of Denmark, is angered by the massacre (his sister has been murdered) so he summons a large army and conquers England. Aethelred flees

▼ **1014**
- Forkbeard dies and is succeeded by his young son, Cnut. Aethelred returns to England and forces Cnut back to Denmark. Aethelred is now back on the throne

▼ **1014–16**
- Cnut's supporters in England rebel against Aethelred; Aethelred's own son joins the rebellion

▼ **April 1016**
- Aethelred dies and his son, Edmund, becomes king

▼ **October 1016**
- Cnut finally gets the better of King Edmund and beats him at the Battle of Assandun in Essex. Cnut and Edmund then agree that:
  - Wessex will belong to Edmund
  - the rest of the country will be run by Cnut
  - when one of them dies, the other will inherit the land.

About a month later Edmund dies and Cnut becomes king of all of England

Chapter 1 Invasion

Britain under Cnut's rule

Although Britain had been conquered by Cnut he saw it as his main domain, rather than part of the Danish Empire. This was because it was his richest kingdom.

Cnut soon inherited the kingdoms of Denmark and Norway; he also ruled parts of Sweden too. All of this – including Britain – is known by historians today as Cnut's North Sea Empire.

Emma of Normandy

Cnut married Emma of Normandy, sister of the Duke of Normandy and the widow of Aethelred. Emma united the Vikings and Anglo-Saxons when she married Aethelred, but for Cnut she symbolised the old and helped him forge his way in England. She brought lands to her marriage with Cnut, expanding his North Sea Empire. Her achievements were not solely linked to marriage; she proved to be a strong leader who was respected and listened to when Cnut travelled his empire. She also improved relations with the Church and helped to bring peace to England. Emma was renowned for being good with money – protecting not only Cnut's but her own interests. Two of her children – Edward (her son with Aethelred) and Harthacnut (her son with Cnut) – became kings of England.

How did Britain change under Cnut's rule?

Good	Bad
• Trustworthy English nobles were left to rule their own areas	• Hostile takeover at the start of his reign
• Peaceful time and free from Viking raids	• He was tough with those Anglo-Saxons he thought might rebel against him
• Brought back the popular and peaceful laws of Edgar the Peaceful	• Ordered the execution of a number of powerful Anglo-Saxons
• Saw Britain as his main domain, rather than a Danish colony	• Transferred riches back to Denmark
	• Danish nobles were given land

SUMMARY

- Vikings started to invade Britain for more land and opportunities.
- Britain was split into areas of control – Wessex and Danelaw.
- The new king, Aethelred, was young and inexperienced and faced new attempts from Vikings to conquer Britain.
- Aethelred offered Danegeld for the Vikings to leave. This became unpopular with his subjects.
- In 1014, Cnut became king and made an agreement with Edmund to share the kingdom.
- Cnut became king of all of England on Edmund's death and gained territories – creating his North Sea Empire.
- Emma of Normandy married Cnut and helped to build a strong empire.

APPLY

FACTORS

a   Write a brief description of the actions the Vikings took when attempting to conquer Britain.

b   Construct a spider diagram to show all the attempts to gain control in England between 978 and 1016. Use two colours to highlight Anglo-Saxon and Viking attempts.

c   Add annotations to your spider diagram to show where Emma of Normandy played a role.

d   **EXAM QUESTION** Was war the main factor in deciding who had control in England up to 1035?

EXAMINER TIP

Emma of Normandy is mentioned in the specification which means the examiner might expect to see you write about her. Remember she was more than just Cnut's wife – how did she help build the North Sea Empire?

REVISION SKILLS

Break down the information about a topic in different ways. You could create a brief fact file, containing two or three important points about the country, person or event concerned.

CHAPTER 2 — A Norman Kingdom and 'Angevin' Empire

RECAP

England and the Norman Empire

Edward became King of England in 1042 after his half-brother – who was Cnut's son – died. He had strong links with the Normans. He did not have any children – so when he died in 1066 there was a rush for the throne with strong contenders willing to fight for England's land and wealth.

The race for the crown

Who wants to be king?

William Duke of Normandy: claimed both Edward and Harold Godwinson had agreed he should take the throne

Harold Godwinson: the most powerful man in England; the **Witan** supported his claim to the throne

Harald Hardrada: Viking ruler of Denmark; stated that as Vikings had conquered England for many years he should be king

Who got to be king?

The day after Edward's death the Witan elected Harold Godwinson as king. They crowned him immediately but that did not stop Hardrada and William planning invasions to take the throne:

- September 1066: Harold Hardrada was defeated by King Harold at the Battle of Stamford Bridge
- 14 October 1066: King Harold was defeated by William Duke of Normandy
- Christmas Day 1066: William Duke of Normandy was crowned king

How did King William control the English?

William faced rebellions which he put down fiercely. He kept control by:

- giving Normans land in return for loyalty and support
- Each Norman **baron** and lord had his own knights and soldiers to keep the peace
- giving supporters top jobs in the Church
- encouraging Norman barons to build castles to control the whole of England

A Norman kingdom

Once again the English were ruled by a foreign power; their land was taken from them and the taxes they paid went to the Normans. William spent half of his time in France to secure his control and power in Normandy, leaving England to be looked after by his barons and lords.

▶ The Norman Kingdom; the Normans didn't try to conquer Scotland, but had a strong influence over it

16 Chapter 2 A Norman Kingdom and 'Angevin' Empire

How did England change under the Normans?

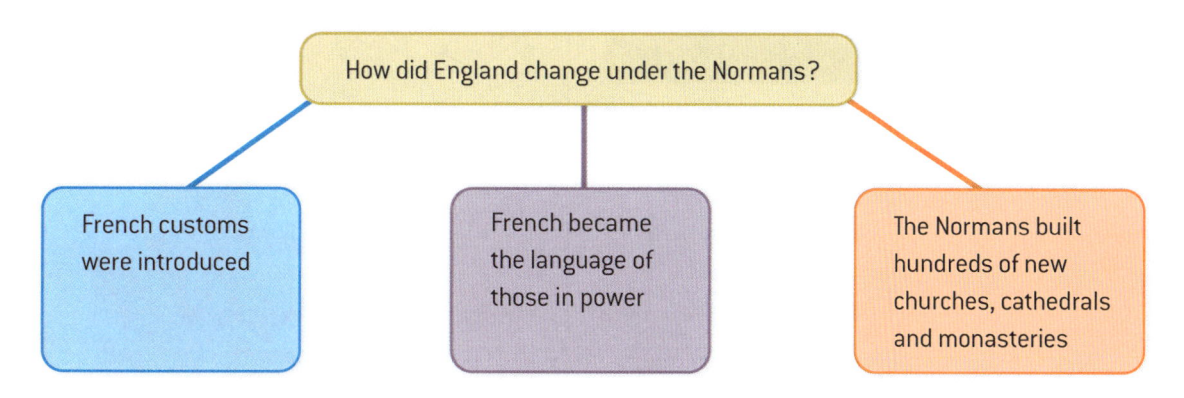

- French customs were introduced
- French became the language of those in power
- The Normans built hundreds of new churches, cathedrals and monasteries

A change of power

William (who became known as William the Conqueror) died in 1087 and the Norman Kingdom was divided up between his two eldest sons. His youngest son Henry got nothing, until one of his brothers died and he became King of England. Henry then went on to defeat his other brother, and so the Norman Kingdom was again united under one man: Henry I of England and Duke of Normandy.

- Henry wanted his daughter, Matilda, to rule when he died. He married her to a powerful French lord, Geoffrey of Anjou
- When Henry died a powerful noble named Stephen seized the throne. Many people felt he had a claim to the throne
- For the next 19 years there was a series of battles as Matilda fought back
- In 1153, an agreement was reached that Matilda's son, Henry, would become king when Stephen died
- In October 1154 King Stephen died and Matilda's son became King Henry II of England

APPLY

SIMILARITY

a List the ways in which England changed after the Norman Conquest.

b Describe how the Normans kept control of England after William's death.

c **EXAM QUESTION** Explain two ways in which the invasion by Sven Forkbeard in 1013 and the Norman invasion in 1066 were similar.

REVISION SKILLS

Use sketches, doodles and pictures to help make facts memorable. You do not have to be a good artist to do this!

EXAMINER TIP

Use 'causes, methods, outcomes' (CMO) to help you structure your response.

REVIEW

Look back at pages 14–15 to help you.

RECAP

The 'Angevin' Empire

Henry and his brothers are referred to as the 'Angevins' after their father Geoffrey of Anjou. Later the family became known as the Plantagenets. Henry II became King of England in October 1154 after the death of Stephen. But he was not just King of England.

Henry's empire

Through land inherited from both his mother and father, King Henry II of England was also:

- Duke of Normandy
- Count of Anjou
- Count of Maine.

After marrying Eleanor of Aquitaine in 1152 he then gained the territories of Aquitaine which spread all the way to Spain. Over the course of his reign he also controlled large areas of France, including Brittany.

Invasion of Ireland, 1166

Most kings had not considered Ireland – which had little wealth – worth invading. However, in 1166, 'King' Dermot of Leinster in Ireland asked Henry II for help against another Irish 'king'.

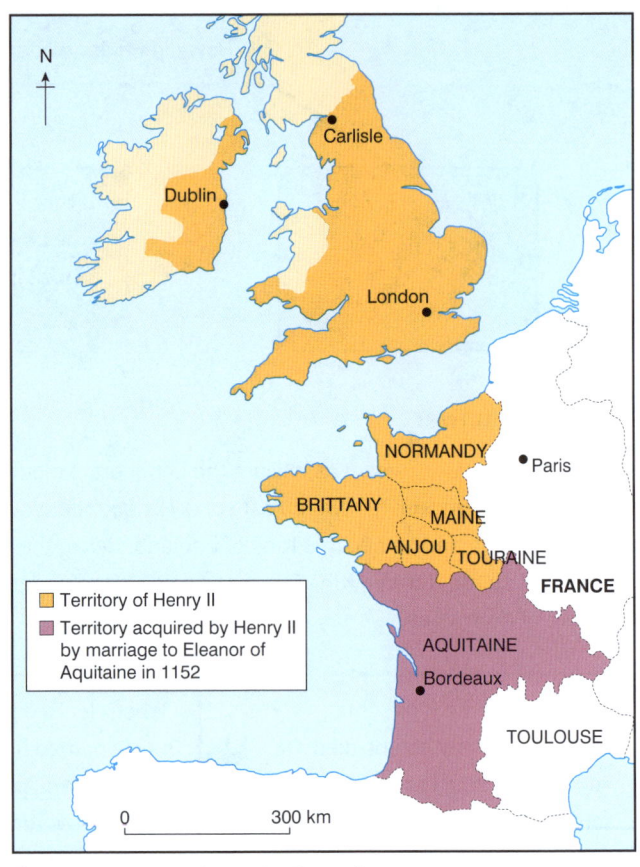

Henry sent an army over to assist but the knights and barons who went used it as an opportunity to seize land for themselves. By the mid-1170s the English controlled more land than the Irish.

Henry used his control in Ireland to strengthen and build new fortifications and to develop Dublin as a centre of trade and commerce. This would give Henry money and extra defence against invading forces.

▲ The Angevin Empire under Henry II

King John loses land

Henry II
Controlled large territories and was very powerful; died in 1189

Richard I
Became king when Henry died. Spent a long period of his reign in France or on **crusades**. Lost land in France to King Phillip II – this was down to John's scheming

John
Became king in 1199 when Richard died. Lost the remaining French land and only held on to Gascony. Became known as 'softsword' because of his poor military reputation

After John became king he had to deal with attacks from those who wanted his brother, Arthur, to be king and from King Phillip II of France. John lost the following territories of the Angevin Empire:

- Brittany
- Anjou
- Normandy
- Maine.

Timeline

▼ 1189
■ Henry II dies and his son becomes King Richard I

▼ 1193–94
■ Philip II of France invades Normandy and Anjou

▼ 1199
■ Richard is killed; his brother becomes King John. John and Arthur of Brittany are in conflict over land in France; Arthur is murdered

▼ 1199
■ The Angevin Empire starts to crumble under John through bad decisions and because he runs out of money at a crucial time

▼ 1202–05
■ Philip II conquers Normandy, Anjou, Maine and Brittany

▼ 1216
■ John dies, and with the loss of Anjou and many other important French lands, this marks the end of the Angevin Empire

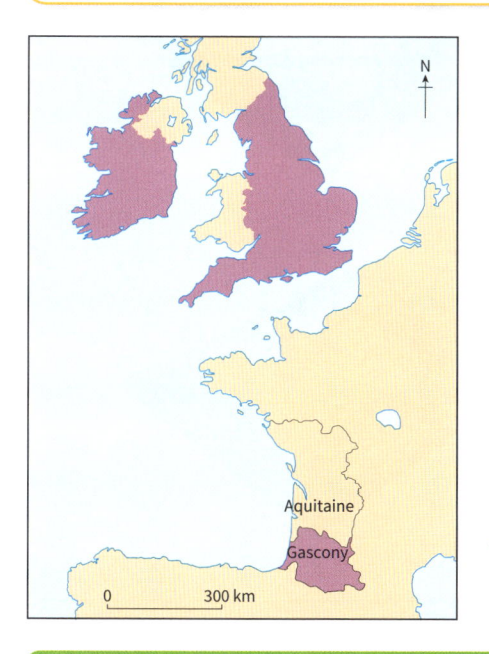

◀ *The Angevin Empire by 1214*

EXAMINER TIP
This activity will help you to plan an answer for a practice question about changing control and different empires. Factors you may consider are war, the role of individuals and economic resources.

Angry barons

John's poor battle record meant that the Angevin Empire was reduced to control of Gascony only

↓

People in England had to pay high taxes to pay for attempted invasions to get French land back

↓

John did not listen to the barons

↓

The barons raised an army against John and occupied London. John needed their support to stay in power so he had to agree to their demands

In 1215 John signed **Magna Carta** which promised to respect the rights of the barons and to stop unfair taxes.

SUMMARY
- King Edward died in 1066 and that opened up the throne to three claimants.
- After the Battle of Hastings, William Duke of Normandy was crowned King of England.
- England remained a territory of the Norman Empire.
- Henry II expanded the empire, partly helped by his marriage to Eleanor of Aquitaine.
- Henry's second son then became King John and lost all the French territories except Gascony; this marked the end of the Angevin Empire.

APPLY

FACTORS

a. Draw a table with the headings in the table below and then populate it to track the reasons for the collapse of the Angevin Empire. Give each event a ranking of 1 (most important) to 5 (least important).

The end of the Angevin Empire			
Event	Individuals linked to it	Factor it links to	Importance (1–5)

b. Use your table to create a mind-map as a plan for answering the exam question.

c. **EXAM QUESTION** Was war the main factor in the collapse of the Angevin Empire?

Britain: Migration, Empires and the People c790–Present Day

CHAPTER 3

The birth of English identity

RECAP

The Hundred Years War

In 1337, King Edward III of England claimed the French throne and declared war on France to protect his economy and power. This is known as the Hundred Years War – it was not one long war, but a series of battles lasting from 1337 to 1453. Most of the fighting was done in French lands.

Causes of the Hundred Years War

Economic
- Edward risked losing taxes as the French threatened to take over Gascony (where wine was made, much of it then sold in England and taxed) and Flanders (where British wool was turned into cloth)

Political
- Edward thought he had a better claim to the French throne than the actual French king at the time
- The French had offered to help the Scots who Edward was in conflict with

Social
- The people of Britain would lose business, such as in the wool trade, and have to pay higher taxes

Stages of the war

The war can be divided into three distinct stages, separated by truces.

Stage 1 (1337–60)
- Edward III won important battles at Crecy (1346) and Poitiers (1356) and gained control of Gascony, Calais and other territories

Stage 2 (1370)
- The French won back some of the land they had lost

Stage 3 (1413–53)
- Henry V became England's king and led the English into the key Battle of Agincourt in 1415. The English forces were tired but luck and good military planning saw them defeat the French
- After the Battle of Agincourt, Henry V went on to conquer Normandy and tighten his grip on France
- After Henry V's death his son took over and the French got back most of the land they had lost
- The French were inspired by Joan of Arc's leadership to take back control of their country

The Battle of Agincourt

The Battle of Agincourt was a turning point in the Hundred Years War.

▲ The first stage of the battle

▲ The end stage of the battle

1. English and French positions at start of the Battle of Agincourt

2. Henry immediately moved his troops forward and ordered his archers to open fire

3 The French tried to charge at the English, but a combination of thick mud, heavy armour, and wooden spikes that the English had set up in front of themselves slowed them down

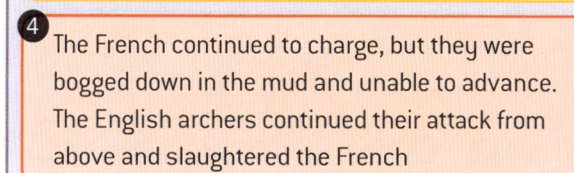

4 The French continued to charge, but they were bogged down in the mud and unable to advance. The English archers continued their attack from above and slaughtered the French

5 The battle was a disaster for the French; the survivors fled

The legacy of the Hundred Years War

Short term
- Some areas of France were devastated with buildings, crops and animals destroyed
- Soldiers and civilians on both sides were killed

Medium term
- France became unified under one king
- England lost money because of lost territories, such as Normandy
- Some English people got very rich from stealing riches from towns and villages
- The foot soldier became the key element to the army
- Gunpowder, canons and handguns were used more in battle
- A new and improved system of taxation for France was started

Long term
- Increased nationalist feeling in both France and England
- The English identity developed – the country began to see itself 'apart' from Europe and as having a common language and homeland
- England looked to conquer lands outside Europe and went on to develop an empire in land further afield

SUMMARY

- Edward III started the Hundred Years War to protect the economy and increase his power.
- Between 1337 and 1360, Edward III regained control of key French territories.
- France began to regain territories from 1370 to 1415.
- Henry V led English troops at Agincourt in 1415 and gained control of much of Northern France.
- By 1453 the English had lost all their territory in France except Calais.
- A national identity emerged in France which became unified under one king.
- The English identity developed with a move away from French influences.

APPLY

EXPLAIN THE SIGNIFICANCE

a Identify two ways in which the Hundred Years War helped to increase English power.

b Describe the biggest change for both England and France during the Hundred Years War.

c Explain how the ideas of national identity that emerged after the Hundred Years War can still be seen today.

d **EXAM QUESTION** Explain the significance of the Hundred Years War for the English identity.

EXAMINER TIP

For higher marks try to show how the significance has changed over different periods or timescales.

REVISION SKILLS

Having someone test you on your notes and revision is an excellent way to see how much you remember, understand, and still have to learn. Brief oral test sessions of about 10 minutes are best.

Britain: Migration, Empires and the People c790–Present Day

Chapter 4: Sugar and the Caribbean

RECAP

Tudor and Stuart explorers look west

In 1496, Henry VII (the first Tudor king) asked John Cabot to explorer further into the 'unknown' world. Later Tudor and Stuart monarchs encouraged more trade and exploration into new lands, laying the foundations for an overseas empire.

The New World: overseas exploration

In the late 1400s, improvements in technology for ships and navigation meant longer journeys were possible, and more ships returned from these journeys.

Individual	Where and when	Key features	Country linked to
Christopher Columbus	1492: the Americas	• Hoped to find new routes to India and China by sea • Sailed west which meant he landed in the West Indies	Spain
John Cabot	1496: Canada	• Sailed from Bristol on behalf of King Henry VII • Found no riches so returned home • Marked the start of the British Empire	England

Piracy and plunder

Early attempts by the British to find gold and create colonies were unsuccessful, but they did establish bases on the North American east coast. From these bases they could explore further and **plunder** riches from Spanish ships and colonies, often using privateers:

- monarchs would grant privateers permission to attack foreign ships and steal from them
- anything taken had to be shared with the monarch
- any sailors that did not share the stolen wealth were known as pirates.

Sir John Hawkins (1532–95)

John Hawkins became a respected English naval commander, merchant, privateer and pirate, and was responsible for building up the Elizabethan Royal Navy. He was the cousin of Francis Drake, another well-known explorer and slave trader.

Hawkins was Britain's first slave trader. In 1562, financed by a group of London merchants, he set sail on his first slave-trading voyage, capturing Africans to sell in the Americas. The trip was so profitable that a second slave-trading voyage took place in 1564, partly funded by Queen Elizabeth I.

The slave trade made Hawkins a rich man. He was knighted by Elizabeth I in 1588.

Why go to the Americas?

- More Britons were willing to go to the Americas after the first successful colony was established in 1607
- There was plenty of land for new 'cash crops' – grown on farms known as **plantations**
- Crops were exported back to Britain for great profit

[Pie chart: Economic factors, Religious factors, Imperialist ideas]

- Some groups (such as **Puritans** and **Catholics**) wanted to escape religious conflict in Britain, so left to find religious freedom

- Businessmen set up plantations in North America and the West Indies
- British investors were keen to develop trade in the Americas because it would help pay for the growth of the British Empire elsewhere
- Exporting and importing within the empire made further profit

Plantation replacing piracy

As Britain's empire grew in North America (and India), and became increasingly profitable, British monarchs stopped granting privateer permissions. By the 1720s, piracy was rare in the Americas. Plantations, rather than privateering or piracy, were where huge profits could be made for Britain.

However, the settlers from Britain found they had many problems with working on plantations:

- hard conditions
- new diseases
- hot weather
- crop failures and food shortages.

This meant that many people did not want to work on plantations so the British began using **indentured servants** for labour. By 1619, however, plantation owners realised they could make more money by enslaving people.

Barbados

The British took control of Barbados, in the Caribbean, in 1625 and it was soon established for tobacco plantations. It was the largest British colony of enslaved people by 1655 and by the 1690s most of the island was covered in successful sugar plantations. Barbados was not seen as a place to settle, but a place purely used to make profit. Slavery was a big part of the profit that the British made there.

APPLY

FACTORS

a. Make flashcards for the different reasons why people settled in the Americas in the sixteenth and seventeenth centuries.

b. Highlight the cards to show push and pull factors (use a different colour for each).

c. **EXAM QUESTION** Were economic factors the main cause of Tudor and Stuart ambitions to claim land in the New World?

EXAMINER TIP

The dates or periods given in the factors question are very important, so it is important to remember to include dates when grouping information into factors.

REVISION SKILLS

Repetition is good for long term memory. Plan revision sessions in short bursts of 20 to 30 minutes several times a day.

RECAP

The move to slavery

By 1619, enslaved people (slaves), mainly from the West coast of Africa, were introduced to British plantations to make them more profitable:

- enslaved people were a cheap source of labour
- plantation owners could buy enslaved people outright, unlike indentured servants
- enslaved people had no legal rights, so they worked without payment
- any children born to enslaved people became their owner's property, further increasing the size of the unpaid workforce.

The development of the slave trade

The idea of slavery was an old one, but enslaved people were used in very large numbers in the Tudor and Stuart periods, especially by countries like Spain and Britain that had started to take over North and South America and the Caribbean.

Enslaved Africans were taken to the Americas and West Indies as a result of a three-part trading journey known as the **slave triangle**:

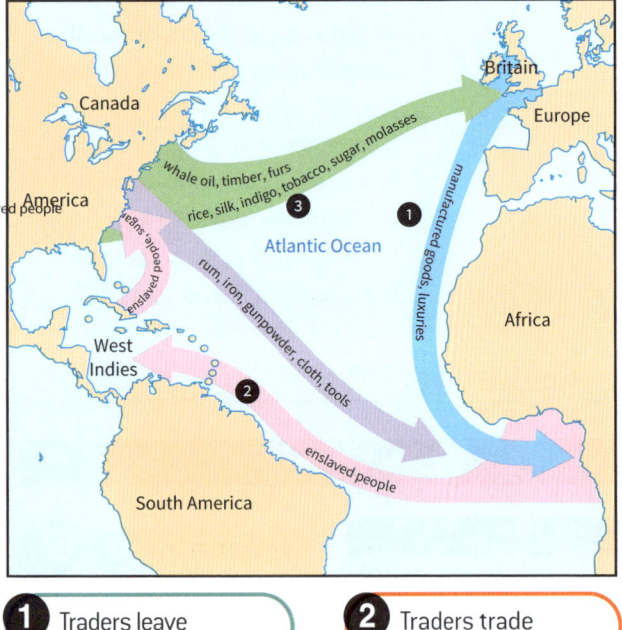

- Those who traded in enslaved people could expect to earn up to 800 per cent on their investment.
- Slave owners also profited as they forced enslaved people to work all their lives without wages and in great hardship.
- Throughout the Tudor and Stuart periods and into the 1800s plantations became more and more profitable.

The impact of the slave trade on Britain

Although Britain was not the only European nation to trade in enslaved people it did make some of the largest profits, and many people were involved at different levels.

1 Traders leave Britain, headed for Africa with ships full of goods

2 Traders trade these goods with African tribesmen in return for prisoners from other African tribes; they also kidnap Africans

3 In the Americas, the enslaved people are traded to plantation owners and farmers for goods such as sugar, cotton or tobacco

Investors: many different people back in Britain, including monarchs such as Elizabeth I and Charles II, gave money and resources to help individuals with the slave trade

Charles II was a partner in the Royal African Company which transported 60,000 enslaved Africans between 1680 and 1688. Many slaves were branded with the letters DY, representing the Duke of York (the future James II)

Involvement in the slave trade

- Shop owners sold sugar and tobacco from the plantations
- Shipbuilders and ship owners allowed their ships to be used
- Workers turned the cotton grown on plantations into shirts
- Dockworkers unloaded ships full of cotton that slaves had grown
- Bankers lent money to the traders

24 Chapter 4 Sugar and the Caribbean

The slave trade benefited Britain in these key ways:

Economic impact

Whether directly or indirectly lots of people in Britain benefited and made money from the slave trade

The British slave trade industry made approximately £60 million between 1761 and 1808

Britain became one of the richest and most powerful countries in the world

Social impact

West coast towns and ports – Glasgow, Liverpool, and Bristol – grew into large cities because of the money made from the slave trade

Many of the fine buildings in these places were built on the profits of slavery

Slavery was so widespread with many powerful people involved, it led to the belief that Europeans were superior to Africans

Enslaved people had been rebelling for years – for example, the Maroons. Some people in Britain now also felt slavery was wrong, and by the late 1700s a campaign started to get the slave trade abolished.

- In 1807 the British parliament abolished the slave trade.
- In 1833 slave ownership was banned not only in Britain but throughout the British Empire.

However, when slave ownership ended in the British Empire in 1833, the government agreed to pay £20 million in compensation to former slave owners for their 'loss of property'.

SUMMARY

- During the Tudor and Stuart period the focus was on the 'new world' as a way to build Britain's empire.
- Privateers were used to help monarchs make money by raiding other countries' ships.
- As the British became established in the West Indies and America the focus moved from privateering to plantations.
- Early settlers setting up plantations quickly moved to using enslaved people.
- Britain made a lot of money from slavery and became one of the richest and most powerful countries in the world.

APPLY

EXPLAIN THE SIGNIFICANCE

a List the reasons why British plantation owners used enslaved people.

b Describe the slave triangle in no more than 50 words.

c Make a mind-map that categorises the effect of using enslaved people on the British Empire.

d **EXAM QUESTION** Explain the significance of the slave trade on the expansion of the British Empire.

EXAMINER TIP

Make sure you make reference to different types of impact, such as economic and social impacts, as well as some longer term results.

REVIEW

For higher marks you will need to mention where the ideas of empire and slavery can be seen later on in history, such as colonisation in North America and the American War of Independence. Go to pages 26–29 to revisit these topics.

Chapter 5: Colonisation in North America

RECAP

British colonies in America

During the Tudor and early Stuart period British settlers started to occupy the east coast of North America, described as Britain's first successful overseas empire. By the mid-1700s there were thirteen established colonies and more and more people started to leave Britain to become settlers in America.

Why did people leave Britain?

Economic factors
- High levels of unemployment in Britain
- Low wages for farm hands and labourers
- Failed harvests caused starvation
- In North America, plantations growing crops such as tobacco, corn, sugar and cotton gave people the chance to make lots of money
- North American seas were stocked with profitable cod

Religious factors
- Christian groups (Puritans, **Quakers** and Catholics) had suffered persecution in Britain
- Failure to attend Anglican services was punishable by death
- In North America different religious groups could join colonies and have religious freedom
- Some religious groups wanted to migrate in order to convert the **indigenous** peoples to Christianity

War
- The **Civil War** in Britain had resulted in increased conflict between religious groups in Britain

Life for early settlers

The thirteen American colonies offered economic and religious freedom but life was not always easy, especially for early settlers.

Where: Jamestown, Virginia

Founded: 1607

Who: Businessmen who were given permission by James I

Why: To find gold and to grow crops

What: There was some conflict between the early settlers and the indigenous Americans whose land they were occupying. Settlers had to rely on local tribes to help them find and grow food. With support from some indigenous tribes, they began to farm the land successfully, with **commodities** such as tobacco making Jamestown a success

Where: New Plymouth, Massachusetts

Founded: 1620

Who: Puritans, arriving on the Mayflower. They would become known as the Pilgrim Fathers

Why: To escape religious persecution

What: Set up their own religious colony with the aims of fishing and trading with other colonies. They worked hard and farmed offshore cod. They established democratic principles and a constitution to keep their Puritan beliefs central to colony life. These rules would become the foundation of modern America

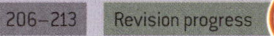

Sir Walter Raleigh (c1554–1618)

- Walter Raleigh was a sea captain for both Queen Elizabeth I and King James I
- In 1584, he was sent to set up colonies in Virginia. He established the colony of Roanoke that year
- The settlers in Roanoke faced numerous problems with their crops and supplies. They came into conflict with indigenous Americans and also caught diseases like malaria.
- Despite the colony being a failure Raleigh is known as the 'Father of American colonies'

REVISION SKILLS

Mnemonics are useful memory devices which can help you recall lists of causes and consequences, or a sequence of events or actions. Identify the key words for the topic. Write them out. Rearrange them so that the initial letters spell something you can remember.

Impact of British colonies on indigenous Americans

The indigenous tribes of North America had been there long before any Europeans. They were mostly nomadic, establishing camps where appropriate. The British were seen as invaders by the indigenous Americans, and today, most people accept that view.

The arrival of colonists from Europe had various impacts on the indigenous Americans.

- Good relations initially existed with some native tribes, but in general the British did not treat them with respect.
- Many tribes were wiped out by diseases that the settlers brought over.
- British settlers attacked their crops and villages.
- In 1500, there were approximately 560,000 indigenous Americans in 'British' territories. However, by 1700, there were fewer than 280,000.
- Many indigenous American tribes moved inland to avoid settlers.
- The indigenous American way of life was wiped out and many adapted to European ways to survive.

Today, indigenous Americans account for only 0.7 per cent of the total population of the USA.

APPLY

SIMILARITY

a List the methods used by the British colonists to keep control of the American colonies.

b Make profiles of the key people and groups involved in the colonisation of America.

c Write a paragraph giving your judgement about the way the colonists treated the indigenous Americans.

d **EXAM QUESTION** Explain two ways in which John Hawkins' contribution to the establishment of Britain's empire was similar to Walter Raleigh's.

EXAMINER TIP

Identify the similarities first, and then write about the evidence for them specifically, for both individuals. Don't tell a story about each one – focus on the point you have identified. Try to find at least two points of similarity.

REVIEW

Go back to page 22 to remind yourself about John Hawkins.

RECAP

The British lose their American colonies

By the 1760s, the British had gained an overseas empire in North America. Many settlers enjoyed the religious and economic freedom that they found in America. It wasn't long until there were ideas among the colonists that they could exist separately from Britain.

Causes of tension between the American colonists and the British

Long term

- Many successful colonists were 'self-made' businesspeople and saw the British class system as outdated. Although most had made their fortunes from plantations and the slave trade they were built on, many believed that anyone could make a success of themselves, no matter what their background
- America had a strong economy that didn't rely on trade with Britain. The colonies traded commodities such as people – both enslaved people and indentured servants – along with other goods. There was a feeling amongst the colonists that they could exist separately from Britain
- The Navigation Acts (1651–73) meant that only British goods could be imported into America. The colonists could no longer trade with other countries
- This **monopoly** of trade with just the British greatly restricted the type and amount of goods that could be brought to America. This meant competition was rare and prices were high

Medium term

- The Americans were ruled directly from Britain yet they had no representatives in the British parliament. They were unhappy at paying taxes without having a say in parliament
- The **Stamp Act** (1765) – this was a tax on the paper used for all official documents
- Colonists were also made to pay taxes to fund the British wars against the French that the colonists felt had little to do with them

Short term

- The Boston Tea Party, 16 December 1773 – colonists poured British tea into the harbour in protest at the tax on tea imposed by the British. The British responded by closing Boston port, causing even more anger
- In 1774, 56 representatives from the colonies met at the 'First Congress' in Philadelphia. A decision was made to fight the British: the War of Independence began

The War of Independence

- The British sent soldiers to force American rebels to stay loyal, but they were met by fierce resistance.
- July 1775: George Washington was appointed leader of the American army.
- July 1776: Congress met again and formally declared themselves independent from Britain.
- Although independence was declared in 1776, Britain only conceded it had lost on 3 September 1783.

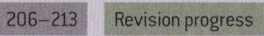

Losing the American colonies

10,000 soldiers and 20,000 sailors died during the war

The war cost Britain around £80 million, increasing its debts. However, rapid industrialisation meant it was still very wealthy

Britain was soon trading with America again, including the slave trade, and they eventually became allies

By 1813, Britain had developed the world's biggest navy which helped defend existing colonies, gain new colonies, and fight existing opponents such as France

Britain was able to focus its wealth and resources in expanding and developing into places like Canada, the Caribbean, parts of Africa, and India

Britain used Australia and New Zealand as the new destination for criminals and as a market for British goods

SUMMARY
- Many groups left Britain to settle in America for religious and economic reasons.
- Early settlers faced many problems but eventually set up successful colonies such as in Virginia and Massachusetts.
- Indigenous Americans were treated badly and pushed off their land to make way for the settlers.
- The colonists who had settled in America started to identify less and less as British and wanted independence.
- The American War of Independence led to Britain losing America as a colony but saw the increased importance of India, Canada and Australia.

APPLY

SOURCE ANALYSIS

SOURCE A
A 1789 painting of the Boston Tea Party, showing Americans throwing the teaship cargoes into the river

a Make a list of all of the reasons the colonists were dissatisfied with British rule.

b Colour-code your reasons – the factors for unrest – into economic, social, and political factors.

c Describe why taxation angered the colonists.

d Study **Source A**. How useful is **Source A** to a historian studying the causes of the War of Independence?

REVISION SKILLS
Write facts on notes and stick them up together in a specific part of your room or house. When you go or look there you will read your notes and associate that part of the room or house with that topic.

EXAMINER TIP
The question references the causes of the war – your answer should directly refer to the changing relationship between Britain and its colony. Use the factors from activity **b** to help structure your answer.

Britain: Migration, Empires and the People c790–Present Day

Chapter 6: Migrants to and from Britain

RECAP

Huguenot migration, Ulster Plantations and Highland Clearances

While the British Empire continued to grow throughout the seventeenth and eighteenth centuries, people were migrating both into and out of Britain. New arrivals helped to shape the British identity and contributed to British life.

Huguenot migration to Britain

France was a Catholic country but it experienced a series of religious civil wars between the 1560s and the 1590s. This resulted in many French protestants – known as Huguenots – migrating to Britain.

Timeline

▼ August 1572
- St Bartholomew's Day Massacre – tens of thousands of French Protestants are killed; many French Protestants migrate to Britain

▼ 1572–98
- Queen Elizabeth I, a Protestant, makes England a welcome place for Huguenots; her ministers invite skilled Huguenot craftsmen to work in England and teach British apprentices

▼ 1598
- French King Henri IV issues a bill of rights for the Huguenots called the **Edict of Nantes** which grants them freedom to practise their religion without fear

▼ 1685
- French King Louis XIV tears up the Edict of Nantes; Protestant ministers are given the choice of converting to Catholicism or migrating out of France. The Huguenots are now officially **heretics** and face persecution once more; about 50,000 Huguenots escape to England

The impact of the Huguenots in Britain

The French Huguenots were mainly highly skilled craftsmen and they had a positive social and economic impact on Britain. They:

- established businesses in communities all over England
- transformed existing British industries e.g. bookbinding
- started up new industries such as papermaking. By the 1710s, Huguenot expertise meant that Britain had 200 paper mills, supplying nearly 70 per cent of Britain's paper market.

Scientists, intellectuals and experts from the community boosted Britain's business, arts and crafts. There was some anti-Huguenot feeling in Britain but the different groups mixed well.

The Ulster Plantations

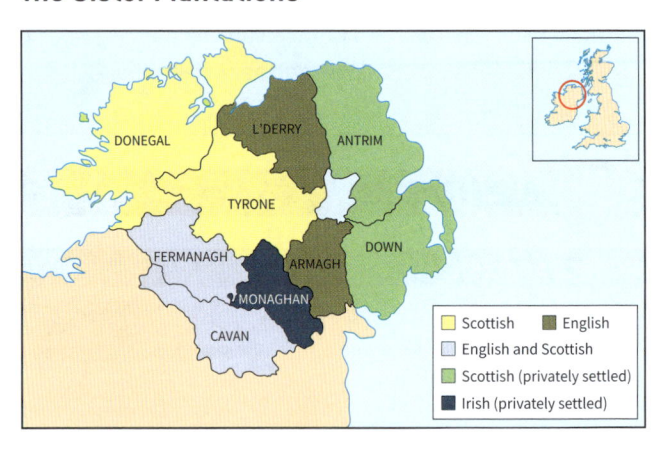

King James I sent Protestants from Scotland and England in the early 1600s to take over land and help keep control of the northern part of Ireland (known as Ulster). He 'planted' the Protestants – believing them to be faithful to him – in a move that became known as the Ulster Plantations.

- Most Irish people resented the settlers migrating out of Britain into Ireland – they saw this as an invasion.
- The population grew rapidly as thousands of settlers arrived, bringing their own customs and religion.
- The resentment between Protestant settlers and the mainly Catholic Irish continued for centuries.

The Highland Clearances

In the early 1700s, over half the people in Scotland lived in 'clans' in the Highlands. Many spoke Gaelic and worked and lived on small farms called crofts. In the Lowlands, towns and cities were growing, and manufacturing and merchants were becoming wealthy.

The Highlanders were largely Catholics and Jacobites, and had participated in the **Jacobite Rebellions** of 1715 and 1745. The Jacobites were defeated at the Battle of Culloden in 1746 and the monarch – George I – wanted to reduce the power of the Highlanders

↓

The English began the brutal policy of removing all potential opposition in the Highlands by getting rid of Scottish chiefs and clans that did not support George I. This was the start of what became known as the **Highland Clearances**

↓

In an attempt to make more money from the land, English landlords moved tenant farmers off the land and set up large scale sheep farming

↓

From the 1780s to the 1820s tens of thousands of Highlanders were evicted from their homes. Some were forced onto barren coastal lands, or on unworkable land where they starved to death

↓

Many Highlanders were forced to move to towns and cities in the Lowlands to look for work, but many more migrated to England and to countries such as Canada and America

↓

Those that left Scotland became known as the Scottish **diaspora** and contributed to the growth of the British Empire

SUMMARY

- Protestants (Huguenots) in France faced religious persecution so moved to Britain in large numbers.
- The Huguenot migrants contributed to British industry and trade.
- In 1610, James I created the Ulster Plantations in an attempt to control the Catholic Irish.
- The Ulster Plantations caused a lot of resentment between Catholic and Protestant communities.
- During the reign of George I the Highland people of Scotland were pushed off their land – in the Highland Clearances – to make way for sheep farming.
- Many Highlanders migrated within Scotland but others migrated to countries within the British Empire where they had a big impact.

APPLY

SOURCE ANALYSIS

a Why did the Huguenots migrate to Britain?

b List the ways in which Huguenots contributed to the British economy.

c Describe Source A. What can you see happening?

d **EXAM QUESTION** Study **Source A**. How useful is **Source A** to a historian studying the impact of the Huguenot community in Britain?

EXAMINER TIP

Remember to connect what you see in the source to other trades and jobs that Huguenots did. Then link the job/trade to economic and social developments.

SOURCE A *Female silk workers in Spitalfields. The industry in East London was founded by Huguenot refugees.*

Chapter 7: Expansion in India

RECAP

British control in India

India is rich in natural resources – iron ore, silk, copper, gold, silver, gemstones, tea, timber and spices. This meant that any country that made strong trade links with India could potentially become very rich and powerful.

Rivalry among European nations

- In 1497, Vasco De Gama (from Portugal) discovered how to get to India from Europe by sea.
- Soon many European countries (including Denmark, France and Netherlands) were sending ships to India to trade.
- European traders set up permanent, well-protected bases along the Indian coast, known as **trading stations**.
- Sometimes the traders lived there with their families. There were often workshops or 'factories' within the trading ports that turned some of the raw materials into goods, such as cotton cloth.

The East India Company

The British trading stations were run by one company – the East India Company (EIC).

- Set up in 1600; had a monopoly over British trade in India
- EIC ships carried cheap British goods and traded them for goods in countries as far away as Japan and China
- Fine china, silk, coffee and spices were brought back to Britain; EIC businessmen, and the kings and queens to whom they paid taxes, made a fortune
- India became an important base for much of Britain's growing global trading
- EIC first set up trading posts in India in Surat (1612), Madras (1638) and Bombay (1668)
- EIC had its own army and navy; local Indian people were trained to become soldiers for the EIC
- EIC's monopoly ended in India in 1694

Timeline

European invasion and trade

- In the 1500s, the Mughals (who were Muslims) invade India and take control of areas mostly run by Hindu princes
- 1658–1707: during the reign of Mughal Emperor Aurangzeb, wars break out across India and the Mughals begin to lose control of the country
- Some European nations take advantage of this and begin to expand their control over India; Dutch, French and British companies, including the EIC, support particular Indian princes with weapons and soldiers in return for rewards such as land or goods; in return, they can then demand rewards from the princes they have supported – perhaps land or goods

The East India Company expands

- In the 1700s, the EIC begins to take more and more Indian land; it uses its private army and navy against various regional rulers of India and takes advantage of divisions between them
- 1757: at the Battle of Plassey, around 3000 company troops (2200 of whom are local Indians) led by Robert Clive defeat an Indian army of over 40,000, led by local prince Siraj-ud-Daula (who is helped by the French)
- This victory allows the EIC to take over Bengal, one of the richest parts of India
- The company also fights against other European nations, such as the Dutch, and takes over their trading posts
- Over the following decades, more of India comes under the rule of the EIC; India is a good place in which to sell their own goods to the many millions of Indians in their territory

The East India Company in decline

- The EIC makes huge profits in India but is losing money elsewhere – mainly as a result of a decline in trade with America
- The British government steps in because it does not want this British company (that pays a fortune in taxes) to go bankrupt and lose control of large parts of India

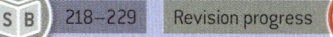

- 1773: the Government of India Act states that both the British government and the East India Company control the territory in India jointly; Warren Hastings is appointed Governor General of India to control the territory
- After Britain loses the valuable American colonies in the late 1700s (see pages 28–29), the British government becomes increasingly involved in India and gradually takes more control of the EIC's affairs
- By the mid-1850s, much of India is controlled by the British

Robert Clive 1725–74

- Started as an EIC office clerk.
- Joined the EIC's army and proved himself an effective and ruthless leader.
- While Governor of Bengal, won the Battle of Plassey in 1757 and oversaw plunder of the region, making a personal fortune.
- Returned to India as Governor and Commander-in-Chief of Bengal 1764–67. His greed and mismanagement increased the devastation of the 1700 Bengal famine, in which about ten million died.
- Criticised by Parliament in 1772 for corruption.

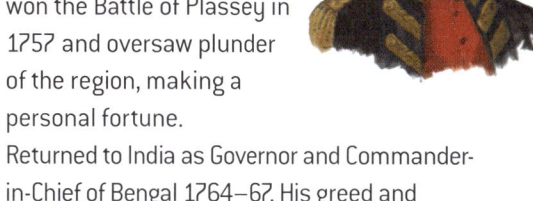

Warren Hastings 1732–1818

- First Governor General of India (1773–85).
- Strengthened British control in India, helping to establish India as part of the British Empire.
- Reorganised tax systems, tightened anti-corruption laws, dealt with thieving gangs.
- Faced accusations of corruption, mismanagement and poor military judgment from political rivals.
- Back in England, faced trial in 1787 over concerns about British standards in India. He was found not guilty in 1795.

APPLY

SIMILARITY

a. Make a list of reasons why you think Britain took such an interest in expansion in India.

b. How did European nations and trading companies exploit internal conflict in India to increase their control?

c. Write five factual sentences about the East India Company. Use a maximum of twelve words per sentence.

d. Create a timeline of how India gradually came under British control.

e. **EXAM QUESTION** Explain two ways in which British expansion in India and British expansion in America were similar.

EXAMINER TIP

Identify the similarity first, and then write about the evidence for it specifically, from both topics.

REVIEW

You will need to remind yourself about the British expansion into America too, so look back at Chapter 5 to help you.

Britain: Migration, Empires and the People c790–Present Day   33

RECAP

Indian discontent

By the 1850s, most of India was ruled by the East India Company (EIC). Many British employees of the EIC in India made huge fortunes and lived in luxury. The British ignored or replaced long-standing Indian traditions, rights and customs. They also replaced the Indian aristocracy. This led to widespread frustration and discontentment.

- British soldiers were stationed in India to 'protect' EIC employees and to help things run smoothly.
- The army also recruited local Indian soldiers, known as **Sepoys**.

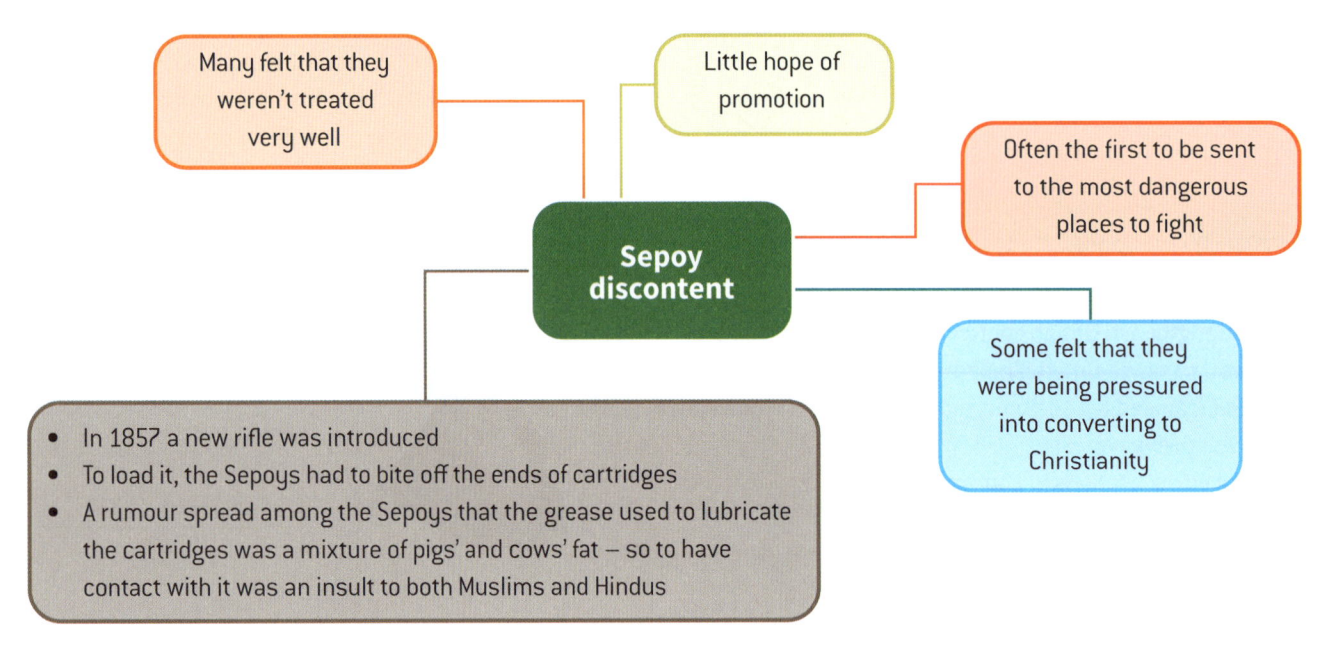

Sepoy discontent

- Many felt that they weren't treated very well
- Little hope of promotion
- Often the first to be sent to the most dangerous places to fight
- Some felt that they were being pressured into converting to Christianity
- In 1857 a new rifle was introduced
  - To load it, the Sepoys had to bite off the ends of cartridges
  - A rumour spread among the Sepoys that the grease used to lubricate the cartridges was a mixture of pigs' and cows' fat – so to have contact with it was an insult to both Muslims and Hindus

The Indian Rebellion of 1857

- The Sepoys objected to the new cartridges, but the British ignored the objections
- 9 May 1857: in Meerut, 85 Sepoys refused to use the cartridges and were sent to jail for ten years
- 10 May 1857: other Sepoys rose up in support of the prisoners and broke them out of jail; British officers were killed and army barracks and the homes of British civilians living in the area were set on fire
- The situation rapidly escalated and many other Sepoys in northern India rebelled

India at war

The events of 1857–58	
The main battles	Fought in Delhi, Cawnpore and Lucknow. The massacre of 200 British women and children at Cawnpore (July 1857) outraged the British. This came to be known as the Bibighar massacre. Back in Britain, crowds cried for blood. The British retaliated brutally against the local population.
The nature of the conflict	Both the British troops and Sepoys acted brutally and there were massacres on both sides. Soon after the massacre at Cawnpore, 70,000 fresh troops were sent to India. The conflict continued for another year.
When did it end?	Peace was declared on 8 July 1858.

Chapter 7 Expansion in India

The aftermath

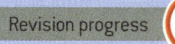

- The rebellion shocked the British – politicians were taken aback by the ferocity of the conflict.
- The British government took over responsibility for running India from the EIC.
- A new government department (the India Office) was set up, and run by a **viceroy**.
- The British were more careful about how they governed – they tried to interfere less with religious matters, for example.
- A limited number of Indians were allowed jobs in local government. A new, professional middle class of Indian citizen emerged, able to use English in addition to their own language, and to learn about new technology and methods of organisation that the British were bringing.
- In time, the Indian Universities Act created universities in Calcutta, Bombay and Madras.

Mutiny, rebellion or war of independence?

- There is no universally agreed name for the events of 1857–58.
- At the time in Britain, it was known as the 'Indian Mutiny' or the 'Sepoy Rebellion'. It is often still called this in Britain today.
- For Indians today, it is most often referred to as the 'War of Independence' or the 'Great Rebellion'. It is looked upon as the first episode in the great struggle against the British for an independent India.

APPLY

SOURCE ANALYSIS

SOURCE A Cartoon of the British response to the massacre at Cawnpore in 1857

a Make a list of causes of the Indian Rebellion of 1857.

b Suggest reasons why the events of 1857–58 are given different names.

c What happened at Cawnpore in July 1857?

d What was the reaction to this in Britain?

e Describe what is happening in Source A.

f **EXAM QUESTION** Study **Source A**. How useful is **Source A** to a historian studying the British reaction to the Indian Rebellion of 1857?

REVISION SKILLS

Making revision cards is a good way of revising and creating a useful revision aid for later use. Jot down three or four things under a heading on each card. Try to include a factual detail with each point.

EXAMINER TIP

It is important to make sure you put the source in context. What was going on at the time? What event is this in response to?

Britain: Migration, Empires and the People c790–Present Day

RECAP

Impact of Empire on Britain and India

The British made a huge impact on India. There is much debate over whether the British had a positive or a negative overall influence. British control in India has often been interpreted differently.

Positive	Negative
• By 1900, the British had built thousands of kilometres of roads, as well as many schools, hospitals, factories and railways. • They also introduced a new legal system and helped settle ancient feuds between rival areas and regions.	• It has been argued that the roads and railways were only built to allow British traders to move their goods more quickly. • British customs were forced on the people and local traditions, culture and religions tended to be ignored. • Indian workers were often exploited, the county's raw materials were taken back to Britain, and native lands were seized.

India's economic resources

- The British made fortunes from trading in India's raw materials, such as tea, gemstones, silk and spices
- Increased trade created jobs for Indians as well as the British in shipping, transportation and sales
- The British introduced an irrigation programme in the Indian countryside, which increased land available for farming
- The British introduced coal mining to India

Building factories

- Many areas in India became industrialised in the same way that British towns and cities were in the 1800s
- Local Indians worked in factories and mills built and owned by British businessmen
- British-made factory goods could also be sold in India

Improved health?

- The British introduced a vaccine and treatment programme to fight killer diseases such as malaria and smallpox, and improved sewage systems and water supplies. As a result, life expectancy increased
- However, there were devastating famines that struck India in the late 1800s, and millions died
- Many blamed the British for helping to cause the famines because they had forced Indian farmers to replace food crops (such as rice and wheat) with high value crops that the British could sell in Britain (such as cotton, tea and oil seeds)

Communications: railways and transport

- The British built over 30,000 kilometres of railways and 130,000 bridges all over India, so goods and people could travel quickly over vast areas and distant parts of the country could be linked
- Canals, roads, factories, mines and farms were also developed (investment totalling £400 million by 1914)
- Some argue that this was done simply to exploit the country and make huge profits, which were taken back to Britain. Others say that the investment created an important legacy that still survives today

Chapter 7 Expansion in India

Culture and society: law and education

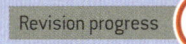

- A legal system was created, based on the one in Britain (the British felt their legal system was the most advanced in the world)
- High courts were set up in Madras, Calcutta and Bombay and parts of Indian law were built into the new legal code
- Hindu and Muslim judges made sure that the British did not forget about Indian traditions and customs when dealing with legal matters
- Thousands of schools and colleges were opened and English language learning spread
- Increased English language learning benefited British traders and meant that Indians had greater access to new knowledge in science, humanities, and literature

SUMMARY

- India became an important base for much of Britain's growing global trading.
- Robert Clive (led British troops at the Battle of Plassey in 1757) and Warren Hastings (First Governor General of India 1773–85) played key roles in the development of the British Empire at this time.
- The East India Company dominated British trade in India. It took Indian land by using a private army and navy against various regional rulers of India.
- By the 1850s, there was widespread frustration and discontentment with British rule among Indians.
- The Indian Mutiny of 1857 led to the British government taking over complete responsibility for running India.
- There is much debate over whether the British had an overall positive or negative influence in India.

Impact of the British Raj on Britain

- British factories brought in raw materials from India, which were converted into finished products in British factories and then sold back to countries in the British Empire, including India itself.
- This created many jobs (e.g. dockworkers, factory workers, shopkeepers) and British businesses made vast fortunes.
- The Indian Army fought bravely and decisively on Britain's side in both the First and Second World Wars.
- Indian tea became a popular drink in Britain and Indian food became more and more common in people's homes. Indian words (such as 'bangle' and 'shampoo') became commonly used, and buildings (like the Royal Pavilion in Brighton) were built in an Indian style.

APPLY

EXPLAIN THE SIGNIFICANCE

a Create a 10-mark fact quiz on the various impacts of the British Empire on both India and Britain.

b Why do you think British control in India has often been interpreted differently? Give examples in your answer.

c **EXAM QUESTION** Explain the significance of British control in India.

EXAMINER TIP

Remember to think about the way India changed over the long term.

REVISION SKILLS

Mind-maps or spider diagrams can be an excellent way of reviewing information. Use colours and small images to make the information memorable.

Britain: Migration, Empires and the People c790–Present Day

CHAPTER 8 — Expansion in Africa

RECAP

The scramble for Africa

In 1870, around 10 per cent of Africa was controlled by European countries. By 1900, European nations controlled over 90 per cent of Africa. Britain was one of the nations that took the most land – 16 areas (colonies) were added to the British Empire between 1870 and 1900.

Why were European countries interested in Africa?

- Africa was rich in natural resources – gold, diamonds and ivory, as well as 'cash crops' such as rubber, coffee and timber
- If European countries controlled huge areas of Africa, they could sell their goods to the people who lived there
- By 1870, treatments had been invented to combat diseases found in Africa such as malaria. This made it possible for Europeans to explore (and conquer) Africa
- This was an era of 'empire-building' where some European countries competed to build large empires. Between 1880 and 1900, they raced to grab as much of Africa as possible before another country got there first. This became known as the '**scramble for Africa**'
- Christian missionaries felt it was their duty to convert people to Christianity. They travelled through Africa preaching about Christianity, as well as setting up schools and hospitals. Europeans often referred to Africa as the 'dark continent', and missionaries felt it was their role to 'enlighten' it

The scramble begins

In the late 1870s, several European nations started to 'claim' land in Africa:

- the French and Belgians began to colonise land in western Africa
- the Germans and the British were interested in the east and the south
- Portugal, Italy and Spain joined in the land grab

To prevent war between the European powers, their leaders held a conference in Berlin, Germany in 1884–85, to decide which nation could take which areas

Little attempt was made to understand the wishes or needs of the Africans themselves. Differences in race, language, culture and traditions were ignored

KEY
- Belgian
- British
- French
- German
- Italian
- Portuguese
- Spanish
- Independent

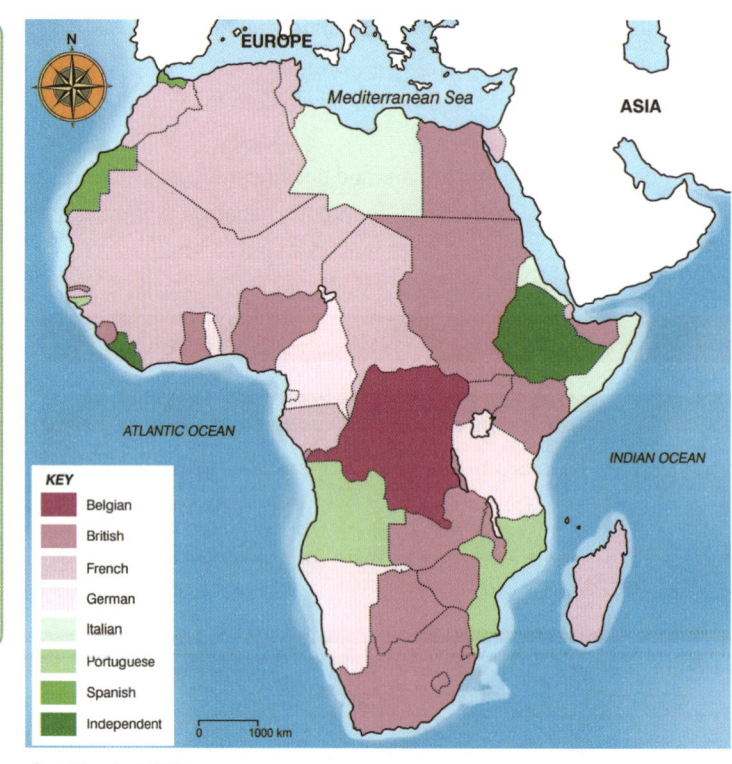

▲ Africa in 1900

The British scramble

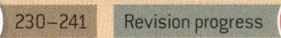

- Britain took over 16 areas of land, including Sudan, Nigeria, Kenya, Egypt and Northern and Southern Rhodesia (now Zimbabwe and Zambia) – 32 per cent of Africa by 1900.
- Britain's land ran in an almost unbroken line from Egypt in the north of Africa to South Africa in the south.
- Britain's control of key areas of African land (in southern Africa, for example) was important because it lay along part of Britain's sea route to India.

African resistance

- African people fought fiercely at times to defend their lands, but the invention of the Maxim gun (a type of machine gun) gave the European armies a major advantage over the Africans.
- Sometimes, Africans won major victories over European countries (such as in the Anglo-Zulu War of 1879), but more often than not the European invaders wiped out the African forces.
- After defeat, many Africans suffered hardship and hunger as their traditional way of life was destroyed. Some were exploited and forced to work as cheap labour in mines, or on huge British-owned farms growing tea, coffee, cotton or cocoa for export back to Britain.

APPLY

SIMILARITY

a Make a list of reasons why European countries were interested in Africa.

b Explain how each of the following contributed to the 'scramble for Africa': political factors (rivalry between nations); economic factors (trade); religious factors (Christianity); explorers; technology; medical progress.

c **EXAM QUESTION** Explain two ways in which British expansion in India and British expansion in Africa were similar.

EXAMINER TIP
Try to find at least two points of similarity and explain them fully, with lots of specific detail.

REVIEW

You will need to remind yourself about the British expansion into India too, so look back at Chapter 7 to help you.

Britain: Migration, Empires and the People c790–Present Day

RECAP

Expansion continues

Cecil Rhodes (1853–1902) is regarded as Britain's most well-known empire-builder, but opinions of him have changed over the years.

Cecil Rhodes and the British Empire

- Rhodes was an **imperialist**, and believed that Britain should extend its power and influence over other parts of the world by any means possible.
- He also believed in **social Darwinism**, which was frequently used to justify European imperialism in Africa and other areas of the world.
- Streets, schools, and two African countries — Southern and Northern Rhodesia (now Zimbabwe and Zambia) — were named after him.

Timeline

▼ 1870
Rhodes moves to Cape Colony (southern part of Africa controlled by the British) to work in gold and diamond mines; makes a fortune

▼ 1881
Elected to the Cape Colony parliament (eventually becoming its Prime Minister in 1890)

▼ 1888
Forms *De Beers*, a company which owns most of the gold and diamond fields in southern Africa; uses his money and political skills to gain control of more land

Cecil Rhodes and the scramble for Africa

- When gold and diamonds were discovered in the Transvaal (an area controlled by Dutch settlers known as Boers) Rhodes was refused permission to mine there. He tried to get rid of the Boer leader, Paul Kruger, by force, but failed. Britain took part in wars with the Boers soon after (see pages 42–43)
- The British eventually won the wars, and gained more territory
- When Rhodes died (1902), statues of him were erected all over the world

Assessing Cecil Rhodes

- Rhodes was a controversial figure when he was alive, as well as today. For example, while a politician, he introduced an act that pushed black people from their lands and increased taxes on their homes
- Rhodes also had many supporters, who argued that he brought vast wealth to Britain and made the southern part of Africa into a more stable and developed place
- In recent years, some statues and references to Rhodes have been removed — he is viewed differently today because we have contrasting views about empire and race to those that were common in previous centuries

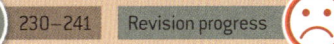

Britain and the Suez Canal

The Suez Canal in Egypt (northern Africa) was an important trade link between the Mediterranean Sea and the Indian Ocean. The route was vital for Britain's access to India (80 per cent of ships using the canal were British).

Timeline

▼ 1869
- The Suez Canal is built jointly by Egypt and France

▼ 1875
- The British and French give money to Egypt in return for control of their trade, railways, post offices and ports

▼ 1882
- Egyptians rebel against British and French interference. The British respond by bombing Alexandria, destroying its defences. France refuses to get involved, Britain sends 24,000 soldiers from Britain and 7000 soldiers from British India to Egypt. Britain takes control of Egypt

▼ 1884
- A religious leader known as the Madhi leads an uprising in Sudan against the British and Egyptians. The rebels kill the British commander, General Charles Gordon, and hold out for many years

▼ 1886–88
- The British, under Lord Kitchener, lead a series of military campaigns against supporters of the Madhi

▼ 1899
- Sudan, like Egypt before, comes under British contro

APPLY

SOURCE ANALYSIS

SOURCE A *British Prime Minister Benjamin Disraeli organised the purchase of shares in the Suez Canal in 1875. This Punch cartoon of 1876 shows Disraeli acquiring the 'key of India' as a result of buying the shares*

THE LION'S SHARE.

a. Why was the Suez Canal so important for Britain?

b. Describe how the canal came under British control.

c. **EXAM QUESTION** Study **Source A**. How useful is **Source A** to a historian studying Britain's involvement in Egypt?

RECAP

The Boer War of 1899–1902

The Boers (descendants of Dutch settlers) were mostly farmers in southern Africa and their colony was named Cape Colony. In 1806, the British invaded and it became part of the British Empire. The Boers left Cape Colony, headed north, and set up two new colonies (the Transvaal and the Orange Free State).

The First Boer War 1867–81

In 1867, diamonds were discovered in the new Boer states. The British tried to get the Boers to unite their states with the British ones, but the Boers refused. A war began, but the British could not defeat the Boers, who fought brilliantly. The British put their takeover plans on hold.

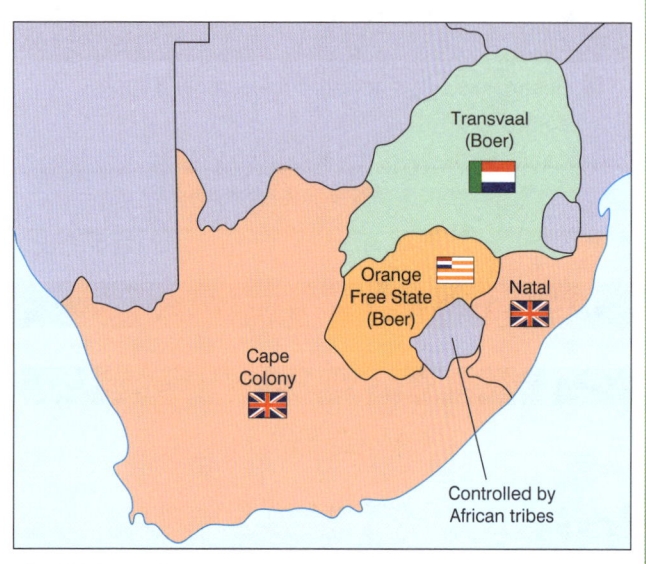

▲ British and Boer colonies

The Second Boer War 1899–1902

Road to war

- 1886: gold discovered in the Boer states
- Cecil Rhodes opened mines inside Boer territory and British workers flooded in
- Boer leader Paul Kruger refused to give the British workers any political rights
- Rhodes sponsored a plan to overthrow Kruger and replace him
- Rhodes' plan failed – and relations between the British and the Boers grew tense
- The British placed more troops along the border with the Boer states
- 1899: another war broke out

Boer victories

- Early in the war, the small Boer army stunned the British with a series of victories
- The Boers were highly skilled fighters, armed with modern guns, who knew the terrain well. They were mobile (on horseback) and 'lived off the land' by foraging for food or capturing enemy supplies. Some black farm workers helped the Boers, for example by moving supplies
- Boers mainly fought in small groups (5 to 12 fighters), so units were hard to detect. They used **guerrilla** (Spanish for 'little war') tactics
- January 1900: the British responded by sending half a million troops, using the latest technology, to fight approximately 50,000 Boer soldiers. Some black farm workers worked for the British, for example as scouts
- The Boers refused to surrender and carried out dozens of small raids on British camps, railways and mines

The British response

- British commander General Kitchener introduced a **scorched earth** policy
- Boer men, women and children were rounded up into concentration camps. Of 116,000 Boers put in these camps, 28,000 (mainly children) died, largely due to disease and illness. There were black concentration camps too – and an estimated 130,000 black civilians (mainly farm labourers on Boer farms) were rounded up – and at least 20,000 died

Peace at last

- By 1902, both sides were exhausted, but the Boers surrendered, and peace talks began
- It was agreed that the Boer states would become British colonies, but the Boers were promised that they could make many key decisions
- 1910: the Boer states joined with Cape Colony and Natal to form the Union of South Africa, part of the British Empire
- This area (commonly known as South Africa) was classed as a **dominion**, rather than a colony, and ran its own affairs

42   Chapter 8   Expansion in Africa

Consequences of the Boer War of 1899–1902

- Britain's biggest twentieth-century 'empire war' was initially greatly supported, but this was short lived

- Around 450,000 British soldiers fought in the war, and nearly 6000 died in battle. A further 16,000 died from illness and wounds sustained in battles

- The Boers lost around 7000 of their 90,000 soldiers, and over 28,000 civilians

- Over a third of British army volunteers were physically unfit for military service – a factor behind the British government introducing measures to help Britain's most vulnerable citizens (free meals and medical checks were introduced for some in schools) as well as the study of nutrition, food and child development. Other measures followed (e.g. unemployment benefit or the 'dole', sickness pay and old age pensions)

Imperial propaganda

- Queen Victoria and her government knew that a large empire meant more trade and wealth for Britain.
- There was a belief that the British – with their Christianity and white skin – were superior to those with different religious beliefs and different skin colours, and had a 'right' to the land they conquered.
- Positive ideas and **jingoism** in relation to the empire were spread to keep the public's opinion of it high and to win their support when taking over more land abroad.
- These positive messages appeared in books, newspapers and magazines (such as the popular *Boy's Own Paper*), in schoolbooks and exhibitions, and on products such as soap and chocolate. Companies were keen to associate their goods with the empire to increase their profits.
- This **imperial propaganda** fuelled enthusiasm about the British Empire. It also often reflected the idea that the British were racially superior.
- The British Empire League and the British Colonial Society were formed to support the idea of imperialism and to promote loyalty to the British Empire.

SUMMARY

- In the late 1870s, several European nations started to 'claim' land in Africa.
- The 'scramble for Africa' saw Britain take over large areas of land, including Sudan, Nigeria and Kenya.
- Cecil Rhodes (1853–1902) is regarded as Britain's most well-known empire-builder, but opinions of him have changed over the years.
- Britain became involved in several conflicts in Africa relating to its expanding empire (including in Egypt and southern Africa).
- Imperial propaganda kept public enthusiasm about the British Empire and British superiority high.

APPLY

FACTORS

a Make a set of revision cards that cover the following terms. Jot down three or four things under a heading on each card:

- the Boers
- guerrilla tactics
- scorched earth policy
- concentration camp
- Union of South Africa

b **EXAM QUESTION** Were economic resources the main factor driving British involvement in Africa in the nineteenth century?

EXAMINER TIP

Try to write a paragraph about at least one other factor, for example ideas such as imperialism and social Darwinism, in your answer.

CHAPTER 9: Migrants to, from and within Britain

RECAP

Irish and Jewish migration to Britain

Some people, or groups of people, move because they want to (known as **voluntary migration**). Others move because they have no choice and are forced to (called **forced migration**). Two of the largest groups to come to Britain in the last few hundred years have been Irish and Jewish people.

Why did the Irish migrate?

From the late 1700s, large numbers migrated from Ireland to Britain, mainly through the ports of Liverpool and Glasgow. By 1861, there were around 600,000 Irish-born people in Britain. Many found jobs in construction as **navvies**, or in mines and cotton mills.

- Most came to escape the extreme poverty in parts of Ireland, and to find better paid work.
- There was a huge increase in Irish immigration after 1846, when a disease called 'potato blight' ruined the Irish potato harvest. Around one eighth of Ireland's population died during the famine. Thousands fled to Britain, peaking in the 1840s and 1850s, when over one and a half million Irish people left their homeland.

British reaction to the Irish

Religious differences
Most Irish people were Catholic – and Britain was a strongly Protestant country. This religious difference could lead to violence, and on occasions angry Protestants attacked Irish areas

Crime
The Irish were blamed for high crime rates in many towns and cities

Jobs
The newly arrived migrants were accused of taking jobs that the locals could have done. In some places, people with Irish accents (or even Irish names) were barred from jobs. When Irish people couldn't find work, they were also accused of being lazy

Disease
Despite getting work, most Irish people lived in terrible conditions in poor areas – so disease was common. As a result, locals would often blame the Irish for causing the disease in the first place. Typhus was even nicknamed 'Irish fever'

Impact of Irish migration on Britain

- Britain's canals, roads and railways could not have been built without the Irish navvies.
- In the early 1800s, as many as 40 per cent of soldiers in the British army were Irish.
- Despite difficulties, Irish migration continued, especially in the 1930s, 1950s and 1960s.
- There were fewer problems between the Irish and the British as they intermarried. Irish 'roots' remain strong in places like Liverpool and Birmingham that had a high Irish population in the 1800s.
- Famous Irish-born people include writers Oscar Wilde and C. S. Lewis, explorer Ernest Shackleton and the military hero the Duke of Wellington.
- Irish literature, music, dancing and bars have become part of British culture.
- According to the 2001 census, six million people (ten per cent of the total British population) had Irish parents or grandparents.

Jewish migration to Britain

Timeline

1290
As a result of religious intolerance, King Edward I expels all Jewish people from England

1656
Jews are let back in to England

1800s
A campaign begins to stop Jewish immigration, supported by key politicians

1847
Lionel de Rothschild becomes the first practising Jew elected to parliament

1850
The number of Jews grows to about 40,000 (out of a population of 18 million)

1855
The first Jewish Mayor of London takes office

1870s
Over the 1870s and 1880s, there is a new influx of Jews from Eastern Europe. They mainly come from Russia, where they are being blamed for the assassination of the Tsar and facing persecution through restrictions and **pogroms**

1874
Benjamin Disraeli becomes Britain's first Jewish Prime Minister

1905
The first Aliens Act is passed by parliament, limiting the number of Jewish immigrants

1881–1914
Around 120,000 Jews arrive in Britain

New Jewish migration in the 1870s and 1880s

- Apart from their faith, the new refugees from Eastern Europe had little in common with the Jews already living in Britain – they were largely uneducated and spoke little English. They worked hard but were badly paid and lived in the poorest areas
- As more Jews arrived, anger and hostility towards them grew, mainly because they were accused of taking jobs from British workers. This has been a familiar theme – like other new immigrant groups, the Jews were unfairly targeted

The Jewish community

- The new immigrants mainly took on three kinds of work – making clothes, shoemaking or furniture-making.
- Jews did very well in these trades – and soon, Jewish communities gained a reputation as hardworking, law-abiding citizens.
- The Jewish community is now a successful and important part of British society. Jews live all over Britain but have particularly large communities in London, Manchester, Leeds and Glasgow.

APPLY

EXPLAIN THE SIGNIFICANCE

a Provide a definition for the following: i) voluntary migration, and ii) forced migration.

b Do you think the Irish and Jewish migrants to Britain experienced voluntary or forced migration, or a mixture of both? Explain your answer carefully.

c Make a list of problems blamed on Irish and Jewish people when they arrived in Britain.

d **EXAM QUESTION** Explain the significance of Irish migration into Britain.

EXAMINER TIP

Remember to think about both the short-term and longer-term impact of Irish migration.

Britain: Migration, Empires and the People c790–Present Day

RECAP

People on the move in nineteenth-century Britain

In the eighteenth and nineteenth centuries, many millions of people moved around the British Empire.

Case study: Africa and Asia	Case study: Australia

• Millions of Africans were enslaved in the West Indies and North America
• There was also an **indenture system** to get large amounts of people to work all over the empire:
  • around half of the immigrants to the American colonies in the sixteenth and seventeenth centuries went there under this system
  • also, millions of Tamils from South India went to pick tea in Sri Lanka, or tap rubber in Malaya
  • over 30,000 Indians moved to Kenya and Uganda to help build railways, bridges and roads. Their descendants went on to play a vital part in the African economies. By the late 1960s there were about 180,000 'Kenyan Asians' (as they were known) and around 60,000 'Ugandan Asians'
  • between 1841 and 1910, around 150,000 people per decade moved around the empire
	• Soon after James Cook claimed the east coast of Australia for Britain in 1770, the British government sent naval commander Captain Arthur Phillip to set up the first colony there
	• Convicts were transported from Britain's overcrowded jails to help him do it. Over the next 20 years, British courts transported over 20,000 more convicts
	• Transportation became very common. It not only removed the criminal from Britain, but it was also quite cheap: the government only had to pay the cost of a one-way journey
	• The punishment had begun in the 1600s when the British colonies in North America began to receive transported British criminals. This stopped when the American War of Independence broke out in 1775; Australia then became the favoured alternative destination after 1787
	• The majority of convicts decided to stay in Australia at the end of their sentences and many became sheep or wheat farmers
	• The settlers treated Aboriginal Australians brutally and their land was taken by force

Leaving Britain

- Over 22 million people emigrated from Britain (left the country) between 1815 and 1914.
- Most went to North America, South Africa, Canada, Australia and New Zealand, hoping to make a better life for themselves.
- Most men found work in building, engineering, farming or mining, while women took up jobs as tutors or maids.
- Thousands went to North America and South Africa to hunt for gold and diamonds.
- 'Free settlers' moved to Australia from the late 1700s.
- Emigration was also used to deal with crime and poverty in Britain. Local councils created schemes for poorer people to emigrate. Other schemes set young criminals up with new lives in Canada or Australia.

Moving around Britain

- Between 1750 and 1900 there was a rapid increase in **internal migration** in Britain. This was an era known as the industrial revolution.
- The amount of people in towns and cities (urban areas) grew much faster than in country (rural) areas at this time (known as **urbanisation**). There were two main reasons:
  - Immigration from abroad: immigrants were attracted to jobs in urban areas (for example, by 1851, 10 per cent of the population of Manchester and 15 per cent of the population of Liverpool were of Irish origin).
  - Rural to urban migration: as farm machinery became more common, fewer workers were needed on farms. Farming is also very seasonal, whereas factory work isn't, so workers in the countryside moved to urban areas to find work.

SB 242–249 | Revision progress

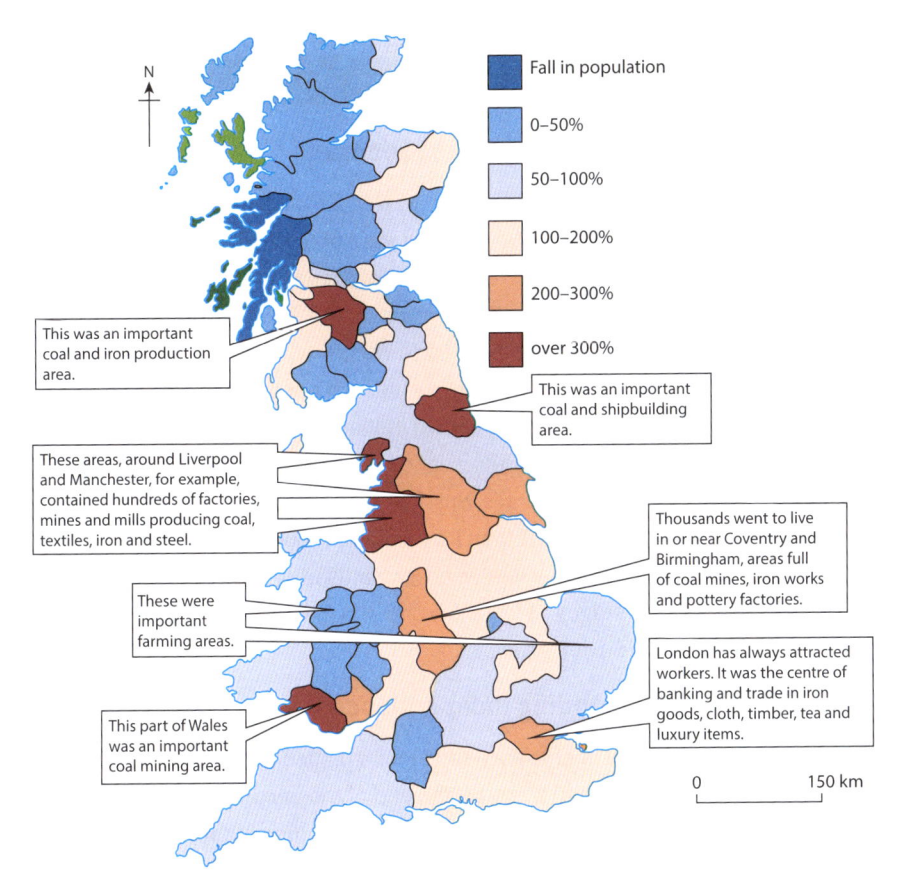

Map key:
- Fall in population
- 0–50%
- 50–100%
- 100–200%
- 200–300%
- over 300%

Map labels:
- This was an important coal and iron production area.
- This was an important coal and shipbuilding area.
- These areas, around Liverpool and Manchester, for example, contained hundreds of factories, mines and mills producing coal, textiles, iron and steel.
- Thousands went to live in or near Coventry and Birmingham, areas full of coal mines, iron works and pottery factories.
- These were important farming areas.
- London has always attracted workers. It was the centre of banking and trade in iron goods, cloth, timber, tea and luxury items.
- This part of Wales was an important coal mining area.

▲ *Population increase 1801–71*

SUMMARY

- From the late 1700s, large numbers of Irish and Jewish people migrated to Britain.
- Most Irish and Jewish immigrants came to escape extreme poverty or persecution, or to find better paid work.
- It was common for criminals to be transported to British colonies in America, and later Australia in the 1700s and 1800s.
- Large numbers of people emigrated from Britain between 1815 and 1914 to places such as South Africa, Canada, and Australia.
- Between 1750 and 1900 there was a rapid increase in internal migration in Britain.

APPLY

SIMILARITY

a Without simply copying the definition from the glossary, write a definition for each of the below from what you have read above:
- forced migration
- indenture system
- transportation
- urbanisation

b What were the main causes of urbanisation between 1750 and 1900?

c **EXAM QUESTION** Explain two ways in which migration relating to Africa and Asia and migration relating to Australia in the 1700s and 1800s were similar.

EXAMINER TIP

Remember that this question asks you to focus on similarities. Identify two things which are similar and explain in detail using facts and examples.

Britain: Migration, Empires and the People c790–Present Day 47

CHAPTER 10: The end of the British Empire

RECAP

Reasons for the end of the British Empire

At its peak, the British Empire covered about one quarter of the world's total land area and contained around 450 million people. Today the British Empire (now called the British Overseas Territories) consists of only a few small areas.

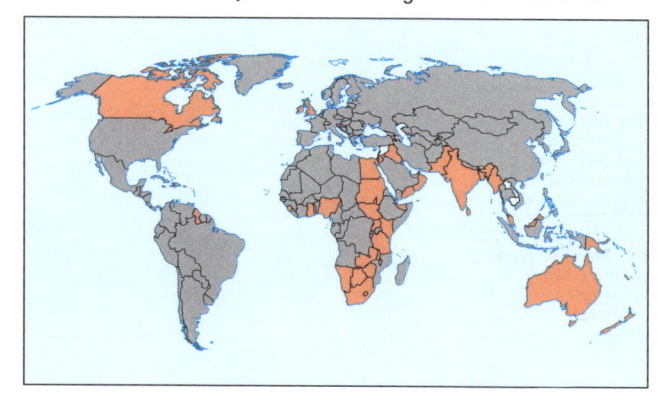

▲ The British Empire at its territorial peak in 1921 (shaded in pink)

The impact of the world wars

- Before the First World War, Britain was a rich industrial power; but after four years of fighting, Britain was in debt. It did recover some strength, but it was then completely bankrupted by the Second World War.
- During the First World War many countries had been cut off from the supply of British goods so had been forced to build up their own industries. They were no longer reliant on Britain, and now directly competed.
- Britain's trade with Europe and the USA became far more important than its trade with countries in the empire.
- Britain was also no longer as important on the world stage — it was now overshadowed by the USA and the Soviet Union.

Demanding independence

Many countries in the empire played an important role in both world wars. By the end of the Second World War, many more British colonies were demanding **independence**. Britain no longer had the military strength or the wealth to hold on to their colonies and many British people felt that rebuilding Britain after the war was more important than holding on to distant colonies.

By 1914, several of Britain's colonies — such as Canada and Australia — were running their own affairs. Some critics of British rule suggested that Britain was more comfortable to allow self-rule in countries that contained a white settler majority rather than 'non-white' colonies such as India or in Africa. They suggested that the British thought people of European descent were superior to non-Europeans

Many Africans and Indians who fought for Britain in the world wars felt they had fought to defend freedom but were getting increasingly frustrated that their own countries were not yet free

Reasons for increasing demand for independence

British-style education systems in some of the colonies (such as India) meant greater access to western ideas like democracy, freedom and **nationalism**. Many people in the colonies wanted these things for their own countries and began to demand independence. In India and other non-white colonies (such as Jamaica), the demand for independence was very strong

Researchers and historians were showing how important the cultures and achievements of Africa and Asia had been before the Europeans took over. Many people in the colonies were very nationalistic and wanted to revive their old traditions, and this could only be done if the British left

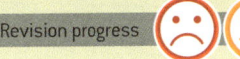

Independence for India

The British Empire took centuries to build up, but only decades to lose. The campaign for Indian independence mainly began with the founding of the **Indian National Congress** in 1885, but Britain largely ignored the demands.

Timeline

1914–18
- India makes a huge contribution during the First World War — providing soldiers, food, materials and finance

1919
- The British make slight changes, but the British government still controls much of the country

1920s
- The Indian independence movement gains more support under the leadership of Mohandas Gandhi

1935
- The Government of India Act gives Indians the right to control everything except the army — but India is still part of the British Empire and is ruled by a viceroy. By now, Muslims in India have formed their own independence group (the Muslim League), and their leader calls for a new separate country for Indian Muslims

1946
- Britain offers independence to India — but the Indian National Congress (not tied to any particular religion) and the Muslim League become involved in a bitter struggle for power. Violence breaks out between Hindus, Sikhs and Muslims. Indian and British leaders agree to partition British India into two states — Hindu India and Muslim Pakistan

14 August 1947
- Pakistan becomes independent

15 August 1947
- India becomes independent

Mohandas Gandhi (1869–1948)

- A Hindu and former lawyer. He led a series of non-violent protests against the British.
- Championed the poor and lived a simple way of life.
- Assassinated in January 1948 by an extremist Hindu, who hated his tolerance of Muslims and others.

APPLY

FACTORS

a Using no more than 15 words per reason, list why there was an increasing demand for independence after the Second World War.

b Create revision cards under the following headings. Jot down three or four things under each heading on each card. Try to include a factual detail with each point.
- The impact of two world wars on the British Empire
- Demands for independence
- The Indian Independence Movement
- Partition in India

c **EXAM QUESTION**: Were the two world wars the main factors in causing Britain to grant India independence? Explain your answer with reference to the world wars and other factors.

EXAMINER TIP

Plan your answer to have at least two paragraphs. One should be on the world wars and a second on another important factor.

REVISION SKILLS

Break down the information for a topic in different ways. You can create a brief fact file containing two or three important points about the different factors that played a role in Indian independence.

RECAP

The Suez Crisis, 1956

After Britain lost India from its empire, the next blow was the Suez Crisis. This crisis had a major impact on the British Empire.

▶ The Suez Crisis was centred around the Suez Canal in north-east Egypt

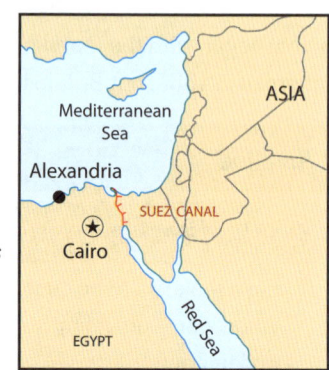

The cause
- In 1956, Egypt's President Nasser took control of the British- and French-controlled Suez Canal
- The canal was a valuable gateway to the Middle East

Invasion and reaction
- When talks failed, British and French troops landed in the canal zone and Israel (an ally of the two countries) attacked Egypt overland
- Both the USA and the United Nations condemned the invasion
- The troops were forced to withdraw and Britain's Prime Minister resigned in humiliation

Impact
- Britain could no longer go to war to preserve its interests if the rest of the world disapproved
- The British decided to allow independence in colonies they felt were stable and prosperous enough to run their own affairs. They hoped that by freely granting independence, they were more likely to have a successful relationship with the newly formed countries

Independence in Africa

The following case studies focus on nationalism, independence and the end of empire in Africa in the twentieth century.

The Gold Coast (Ghana): March 1957	
Build-up to independence	Role of individuals
• 1920s: An independence campaign began in West Africa. The National Congress of British West Africa asked the British government for more control of their own affairs, but the request was rejected • 1940s: There were large independence movements in several African nations including the Gold Coast • The British felt it was important that any new countries in the region were stable and democratic • The Gold Coast was one of the most stable and prosperous countries in the region. Its key independence leader, Dr Kwame Nkrumah, campaigned hard for the British to leave – he was thrown in jail several times by the British colonial authorities • 1951: Nkrumah won the Gold Coast elections, even though he was still in jail. On his release, he was allowed to become Prime Minister – but the Gold Coast remained part of the British Empire • 1956: Nkrumah was re-elected, and the British took this as a sign that they should leave	Kwame Nkrumah (1909–72) • Had a troubled time as Ghana's leader. Ghana became a republic in 1960, and Nkrumah was elected President. There were fierce rivalries between him and other political leaders and there was an attempted assassination in 1962 • He dealt harshly with groups that opposed his rule. The economy declined in the early 1960s and the army and the police seized control in 1966. Nkrumah fled to nearby Guinea and later Romania

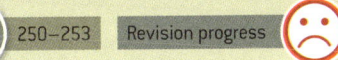

Kenya: 12 December 1963	
Build-up to independence	Role of individuals
<ul><li>1940s: Several independence groups formed. The Kenya African Union (KAU) and its leader, Jomo Kenyatta, campaigned for both independence and access to white-owned land</li><li>Another group, known as the Mau Mau, violently resisted colonial rule. In the 1950s, the British fought the Mau Mau with their own violent campaign</li><li>Many Kenyan independence leaders (including those with no connection to the Mau Mau, such as Kenyatta) were arrested and jailed</li><li>Many white settlers later chose to leave Kenya</li><li>The **Mau Mau Rebellion** lasted for over eight years and eventually persuaded the British that reforms were necessary</li><li>On 12 December 1963, Kenya gained its independence from Britain; Kenyatta, who had been released from prison in 1961, became Prime Minister</li><li>In 2013, the British government apologised for the way it had dealt with the Mau Mau Rebellion and agreed to pay compensation</li></ul>	Jomo Kenyatta (1891–1978)<ul><li>In 1947, was elected President of the Kenya African Union (KAU) and campaigned for independence</li><li>Was accused of being a member of the Mau Mau and imprisoned from 1953 to 1961</li><li>Became Kenya's Prime Minister (1963) and later President (1964). He dealt harshly with groups that opposed his rule – and eventually banned opposition parties</li></ul>

SUMMARY

- By 1914, several of Britain's colonies were running their own affairs.
- By the end of the Second World War, many more British colonies were demanding independence, including India.
- The Suez Crisis in Egypt showed that Britain could no longer go to war to protect trade and its empire if the rest of the world disapproved.
- After long and sometimes bitter campaigns, colonies such as India and countries such as Kenya became independent.

APPLY

SIMILARITY

a Create revision cards for each of the case studies on these pages. Try to make your notes from memory to begin with, before checking them against the revision guide for accuracy. Jot down three or four things under a heading on each card. Try to include a factual detail with each point.

b Identify some similarities and differences between independence in India, the African Gold Coast and Kenya.

c **EXAM QUESTION** Explain two ways in which the decline of British control in India and the decline of British control in Africa were similar.

EXAMINER TIP

Identify the similarities first, and then write about the evidence for them specifically, from both topics. Identify two points of similarity.

REVISION SKILLS

Mind-maps or diagrams are a good way of connecting different pieces of information. Draw lines between people or events and write on that line why or what links them.

CHAPTER 11 The legacy of the British Empire

📖 RECAP

Immigration to Britain after the Second World War

There were two main reasons why large groups of immigrants came to Britain after 1945:
- some came as refugees from war-torn Europe
- other migrants came from parts of the British Empire to find work.

Ireland

When? Many generations had come before 1945. Further arrivals in the 1950s and 1960s

Why? Some came to join families; others came to look for work, and to escape poverty and hardship in Ireland. By 2001, around six million people (ten per cent of the total British population) had Irish parents or grandparents

West Indies

When? Thousands moved to Britain during the war (but most returned home). Many arrivals from 1948 to 1970

Why? Encouraged to come because of a labour shortage; some came because of unemployment and poverty at home in places such as Jamaica and Barbados

Cyprus

When? During the 1950s, and then further arrivals in the 1970s

Why? Initially as a result of tension and violence on the island. Cyprus became an independent country in 1960, but when Turkey invaded and divided the island in two in the 1970s, there were further arrivals

Europe

When? Mainly from the 1930s to the 1950s

Why? Around 60,000 German Jews fled the Nazis in the 1930s. Thousands of Poles came during the war – and by 1950, around 100,000 Hungarians, Ukrainians, Yugoslavs, Estonians, Latvians and Lithuanians had fled from Russian rule

East Asia

When? During the 1950s and 1960s, from the British colony of Hong Kong, and British-controlled Malaysia and Singapore

Why? Most came to look for work, and to escape poverty and hardship. In 1997, Hong Kong stopped being a British colony and became part of China. Around 50,000 people from Hong Kong were given British passports at this time

South Asia

When? In the late 1940s and 1950s

Why? Some fled the violence and fighting during the time when India was partitioned. By 1955, around 10,000 people had moved to Britain, looking for work and better education opportunities

West Africa

When? In the late 1940s onwards

Why? British West Africans (from what is now Nigeria, The Gambia, Sierra Leone and Ghana) moved to Britain to find work and to get a better standard of education than was available in their own countries

Kenya and Uganda

When? In the 1960s and 1970s

Why? Around 70,000 Kenyan and Ugandan Asians moved to Britain from their homes in Africa. They had originally moved to Africa from India and Pakistan, when these nations were part of the British Empire, but when Kenya and Uganda became independent from Britain, the new governments decided to drive them out, so many came to Britain to escape racist attitudes and intolerance

Idi Amin (c1925–2003)

- Rose within the British colonial army from the 1940s onwards and made the highest rank possible for a black African.
- Served with the British in the Mau Mau Rebellion in Kenya.
- Overthrew the Ugandan leader in 1971 and declared himself president. Lived a lavish lifestyle.
- Stayed in power at all costs – often by violating human rights via mass killings, for example.
- Expelled all Asians from Uganda in 1972, contributing to the breakdown of Uganda's economy.
- Overthrown in 1979 – fled to Libya then to Saudi Arabia.

Britain's changing attitude to immigration

As immigration to Britain increased, some politicians with extreme anti-immigration views gained some support, but racist political parties remained fairly small.

In the 1960s, the government tried to slow down the number of black and Asian people entering Britain.

- In 1962, an Immigration Act said that any black or Asian person wanting to enter the country must have a skilled job already lined up – and a limit was put on the number of immigrants allowed in.
- However, no limits were put on Irish immigrants or any other white minority ethnic groups, such as Australians.
- In 1968, when the government feared a large number of Kenyan Asian arrivals into Britain, the Commonwealth Immigrants Act was created. This said that Kenyan Asians with British passports were no longer allowed to enter the country – but white Kenyans with British passports were.
- These policies divided the country. They were welcomed by some, while others felt that the laws were racist.

APPLY

SOURCE ANALYSIS

▶ **SOURCE A** *A cartoon created by Victor Weisz for the Evening Standard, 1961; the caption reads, 'The Commonwealth can be an example to other nations' and is a quote from Prime Minister Harold Macmillan to the Commonwealth Parliamentary Conference, where the government discussed the Commonwealth Immigrants Act*

a Describe Source A. What can you see happening?

b What message is the cartoonist of Source A trying to convey?

c Why was this cartoon drawn in 1961?

d Write a paragraph describing the links between the features of Source A to government acts about immigration.

e Study **Source A**. How useful is **Source A** to a historian studying government responses to immigration in the twentieth century?

EXAMINER TIP

Try to link what you can see in the source with your own knowledge of the situation surrounding immigration at this time.

RECAP

The Commonwealth

Nearly all former colonies of the British Empire now belong to an organisation called the 'Commonwealth of Nations'.

- It promotes democracy, human rights, good government, fair laws and world peace in the nations that were formerly controlled by Britain.
- Each country has close cultural, trade and sporting links to Britain.
- In 1948, the British Nationality Act was passed. All who lived within the British Empire – the Commonwealth – were British passport holders and entitled to live and work in Britain.

Empire Windrush and the Caribbean migrants

In June 1948, a ship named *Empire Windrush* brought the first of many migrants from the Caribbean (known as the West Indies) to the UK. Thousands more followed between 1948 and 1971, from islands that were part of the British Empire (such as Jamaica and Trinidad and Tobago). These migrants have been called the 'Windrush generation'.

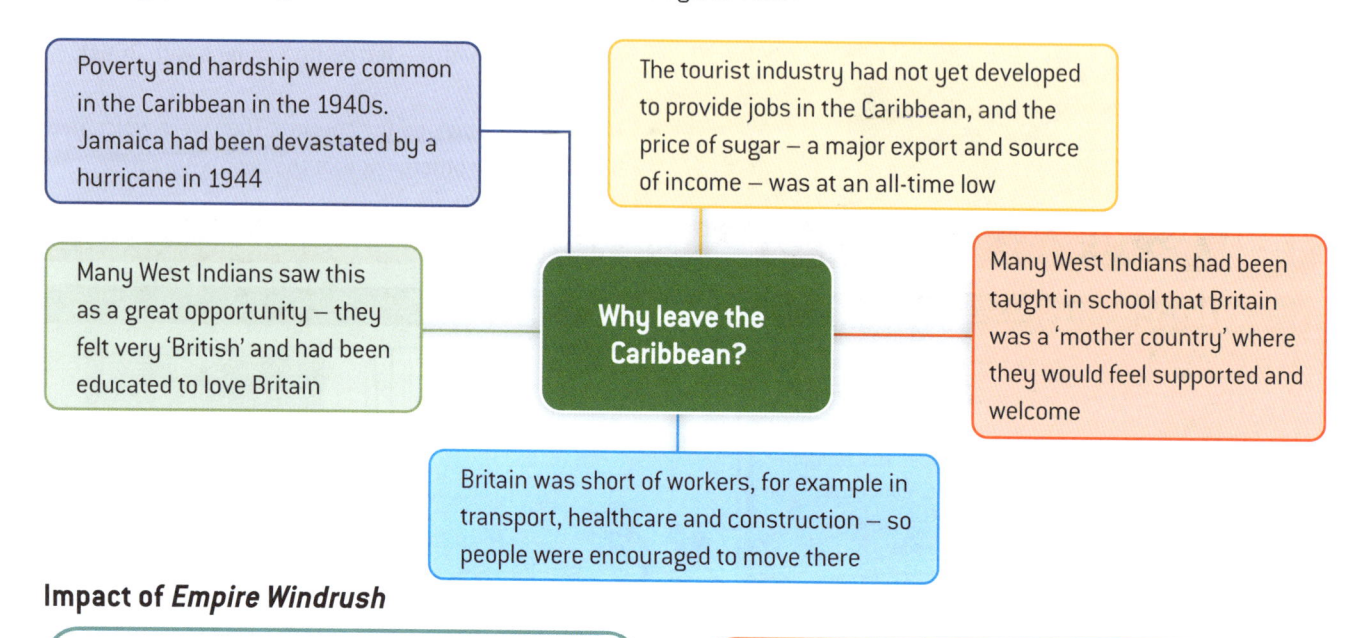

Why leave the Caribbean?

- Poverty and hardship were common in the Caribbean in the 1940s. Jamaica had been devastated by a hurricane in 1944
- The tourist industry had not yet developed to provide jobs in the Caribbean, and the price of sugar – a major export and source of income – was at an all-time low
- Many West Indians saw this as a great opportunity – they felt very 'British' and had been educated to love Britain
- Many West Indians had been taught in school that Britain was a 'mother country' where they would feel supported and welcome
- Britain was short of workers, for example in transport, healthcare and construction – so people were encouraged to move there

Impact of *Empire Windrush*

- Newspapers carried stories of the 'colour problem' that was heading towards Britain, and some politicians demanded that the ship should be turned around and sent back
- Not all white Britons welcomed the immigrants. Some were suspicious of people of another race and culture, while others feared they would lose their jobs to the immigrants
- Some immigrants found good jobs, but many – whatever their qualifications – worked in low-paid jobs as cleaners and hospital porters
- They experienced difficulties finding decent places to live. Often, they would be faced with openly racist words and attitudes. These attitudes that prevented black and other minority ethnic groups from renting houses and getting jobs became known as the 'colour bar'
- Despite the problems, many thousands decided to stay in Britain. By 1960, there were around 40,000 West Indian immigrants arriving each year

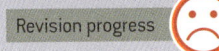

The work of Claudia Jones (1915–64)

- Born in Trinidad, she moved to New York as a child.
- Worked on newspapers and magazines; championed democracy, equal rights for African Americans, and safe working conditions.
- Was considered an extreme radical in America because of her views and was deported; gained **asylum** in Britain in 1955.
- In 1958, became founder and editor of the first black British weekly newspaper, *The West Indian Gazette,* which she used in her fight for equality.
- There were occasional outbreaks of violence in areas where large numbers of West Indians lived. In 1958, in Nottingham and in Notting Hill, London, white youths attacked black youths.
- Following the Notting Hill and Nottingham race riots in 1958, Jones helped launch an annual 'Mardi Gras' event in 1959, aimed at showing the culture and talent of the Caribbean to the people of Britain. This later became the Notting Hill Carnival, one of the largest street festivals in the world.

APPLY

SOURCE ANALYSIS

SOURCE A Jamaican men in a street in Brixton, south London, in the 1960s; the racist graffiti on the wall stands for 'Keep Britain White'

a List reasons why:
- people may have wanted to leave the Caribbean at the end of the Second World War
- people from the Caribbean may have chosen to move to Britain
- people from the Caribbean believed they had a right to live in Britain in the 1940s and 1950s.

b What was the *Empire Windrush*?

c Study **Source A**. How useful is **Source A** to a historian studying the reaction in Britain to Caribbean migrants?

EXAMINER TIP

Try to link what you can see in the source with your own knowledge of the situation surrounding immigration at this time.

RECAP

The Falklands War, 1982

Several colonies have remained part of the British Empire. One of these colonies is a group of islands in the southern Atlantic Ocean, off the east coast of Argentina, called the Falkland Islands. In 1982, Britain fought a war to defend these islands when Argentina invaded.

The colony

- Over 700 islands, located about 300 miles off the coast of Argentina
- Britain first claimed the islands in 1765, but the Spanish later took them over and named them the Islas Malvinas
- Claimed by Argentina when Spanish rule ended in 1806
- Britain seized the uninhabited islands from Argentina in 1833, and British settlers began to live there – the majority of the population of around 2000 are of British descent

Cause of conflict

- From the time that Britain took control there has been a long, heated argument between Argentina and Britain
- In the early 1980s, Argentina was controlled by the army and its leader, General Galtieri
- The Argentinian economy was having severe problems and Galtieri hoped that a successful war (ending with the return of the Falklands) would restore national morale and belief in his government

The invasion

- 2 April 1982: Around 12,000 Argentine troops invaded the islands and quickly took control
- As well as the Falklands, Argentina also attacked the British-controlled islands of South Georgia and the South Sandwich Islands
- Many of Argentina's troops were new recruits who were poorly trained
- Most South American countries (except Colombia and Chile) supported Argentina's invasion and its claim to the islands

The British response

- Britain's Prime Minister, Margaret Thatcher, responded quickly and defiantly to the invasion
- She received near universal support from politicians and the British public, and plans to re-take the Falklands took shape quickly
- Britain sent a task force of over 100 ships and around 28,000 troops to the islands, and declared a 320-kilometre **exclusion zone** around them
- It was not a long conflict. It ended on 14 June when the Argentines surrendered

The impact of the Falklands War

Short term

- 255 British and 750 Argentinian troops were killed
- The British lost six ships (ten others were damaged), 34 aircraft and over £2.5 billion was spent

Medium term

- Boost in patriotic feeling among British citizens, who were proud of their country's defence of one of its last colonies
- Before the war, Thatcher had been criticised because unemployment was high, some industries were struggling and there were government spending cuts. The victory boosted the popularity of Thatcher – and played a role in her re-election in 1983
- After the loss, President Galtieri was forced to resign, paving the way for a new, democratic government in Argentina

Chapter 11 The legacy of the British Empire

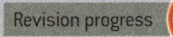

Long term

- The relationship between Britain and the USA became stronger
- Foreign politicians reported that there was an increase in international respect for Britain, which had been regarded as a fading world power
- The war did not end the dispute between Argentina and Britain. Argentina continues to claim the islands, but Britain maintains that this is not open to negotiation
- To this day, Argentinians refer to the islands as Islas Malvinas – and around 1000 British troops are posted there

SUMMARY

- Large groups of immigrants came to Britain after 1945, mainly as refugees from war-torn Europe, or from parts of the British Empire to find work.
- In the 1960s and 1970s, around 70,000 Kenyan and Ugandan Asians moved to Britain from their homes in Africa.
- Nearly all former colonies of the British Empire now belong to an organisation called the 'Commonwealth of Nations'.
- In June 1948, the *Empire Windrush* brought the first of many migrants from the West Indies to the UK. Thousands more followed between 1948 and 1971, and the migrants have been called the 'Windrush generation'.
- In 1982, Britain fought (and won) a war to defend the Falkland Islands when Argentina invaded.

APPLY

SOURCE ANALYSIS

SOURCE A A June 1982 photograph from the Liverpool Echo, a local Liverpool newspaper that supported the South Atlantic Appeal Fund. The Fund was set up to raise money for British victims of the Falklands War and their families. Many in the city of Liverpool did not support Thatcher's government at this time, blaming it for factory closures and high unemployment rates in the area.

a Where are the Falkland Islands?

b List as many reasons as you can to explain why Argentina invaded the Falkland Islands.

c Divide the list into long-term and short-term reasons.

d In your own words, write down an example of a short-, medium- and long-term impact of the Falklands War.

e **EXAM QUESTION** Study **Source A**. How useful is **Source A** to a historian studying Britain's response to Argentina's invasion of the Falkland Islands in 1982?

EXAMINER TIP

To obtain a higher level, link what you can see in the source to your own knowledge of the invasion.

REVISION SKILLS

Create a 10 point fact test to test your basic, core knowledge about a topic. You can swap the test with a friend.

Chapter 12: Britain's relationship with Europe

RECAP

Britain and Europe

After the Second World War, European leaders were determined to avoid another large-scale war, and felt that differences should be put aside. They joined forces to develop Europe peacefully. It was felt a strong, unified Europe might become a powerful trading group and a competitor for the powerful and influential USA.

Britain did not join the group (ECSC, later the EEC) to begin with because it still had strong ties with countries in the British Empire, and those that had gained independence. Britain was also closely linked with the USA.

In the early 1960s, many more countries began to gain their independence from Britain and it was clear that the EEC was becoming an economic success.

The British public has long been divided over its relationship with the rest of Europe:

- those in favour of Britain having a close relationship (pro-Europeans) believe that the country benefits from the strong trade links and 'collective security'
- those against it (Eurosceptics) argue that Britain is unique and should be free to make all its own decisions.

End of the Cold War and membership of the European Union

Timeline

1951
- Six countries (France, West Germany, Italy, Belgium, the Netherlands and Luxembourg) join their coal and steel industries together to form the European Coal and Steel Community (ECSC). That way, they can never build up their armies on their own, and without the other countries finding out

1957
- The ECSC is renamed the European Economic Community (EEC). Members agree to cooperate in producing nuclear power

1968
- The EEC begins to trade with other countries as a single group – the biggest trading organisation in the world

1973
- Britain, Denmark and Ireland are admitted into the EEC

1975
- A UK referendum is held to decide whether Britain should remain part of the EEC. The result is two to one in favour of staying in

1979
- The European Parliament is elected by EEC citizens. At first it can just advise, but later it can pass laws that apply in all member countries

1992–93
- The Maastricht Treaty is signed, which renames the community as the European Union (EU). All countries agree to cooperate even further, in issues such as foreign affairs and security. The EU formalises the **single market**

2002
- Twelve member countries adopt new Euro notes and coins as their currency

2004
- The USSR's influence and control over many countries in Eastern Europe had stopped at the end of the Cold War (early 1990s); many of these newly independent nations wanted to become EU members, and in 2004, eight of them join

2007–13
- Romania, Bulgaria and Croatia join, bringing total membership to 28

2016
- A UK referendum is held again. The result is 52 per cent to 48 per cent to leave the EU

2020
- The UK leaves the EU

Migration in Europe

Being a part of the EU means there is free movement of workers – EU citizens can work in any other EU member state on the same conditions as the citizens of that state. Every year, numerous Europeans move between European countries. Europe is also a popular destination for people who do not live in the EU – individual countries can decide how many non-EU citizens they will admit.

Migration within the EU	Migration from outside the EU
• In the 1970s, around 20,000 EU citizens entered Britain every year, rising to about 60,000 per year by the early 2000s • In 2004, eight more countries joined the EU, including Eastern European nations such as Poland and Hungary. In two years, around 600,000 Eastern European immigrants came to Britain. Most migrated to look for work and better pay • Many found jobs in the construction and retail industries, often earning five times as much as they did in their home countries	• After the Second World War, immigration was encouraged, so many immigrants came from current or former countries of the British Empire • Britain tightened immigration controls in the 1970s • Britain now operates a points-based system for non-EU immigrants. Applicants are awarded points depending on their skills, education, income and age. If an applicant reaches a certain total of points, then they are given a visa to enter Britain to work • Britain also gives permission for thousands of non-EU citizens to study at colleges and universities • In recent years, a growing number of refugees have come into the EU from war-torn countries like Afghanistan, Iraq and Syria. Many governments (including in Britain) have restricted refugee access but the EU is working on a new long-term approach to migration for asylum seekers.

Net migration figures fluctuate over time. People emigrate for all sorts of reasons, including a better job, a better climate or more opportunities.

People have different opinions about the impact of migration on Britain:

- some believe that immigration damages community relations, and that there is great public anxiety over issues such as pressure on public services
- others argue that most immigrants are young and able, so they work and pay more in taxes, use less of the public healthcare and education services, and help with the economic growth of the country.

SUMMARY

- A strong, unified group of countries formed a powerful trading group in Europe, now known as the EU.
- Britain's involvement in the EU has always divided opinions.
- EU citizens can work in any other EU member state on the same conditions as the citizens of that state.
- Thousands of non-EU citizens migrate to Britain.
- People have different opinions about the impact of migration on Britain.

APPLY

FACTORS

a Make a list of reasons why people have settled in Britain in the twentieth century.

b **EXAM QUESTION** Has war been the main factor in causing population movements in the twentieth century? Explain your answer with reference to war and other factors.

REVIEW

Look back at the many reasons why people have settled in Britain in the twentieth century. You will find lots of these reasons on pages 52–53.

EXAMINER TIP

Always write about the given factor and then compare it to another two. For higher level answers you should try to compare all of the factors in order to give a judgement on which one is the most important.

Exam practice

GCSE sample answers

REVIEW

On these exam practice pages, you will find a sample student answer for each of the exam questions for Paper 2 Britain: Migration, Empires and the People Thematic Study. What are the strengths and weaknesses of the answers? Read the following pages and think carefully about what the student has written, what the examiner has said about each answer, and how you might improve your own answers to the Migration, Empires and the People questions.

The source analysis question

▼ **SOURCE A** *A map from 1902 showing the extent of the British Empire. The Latin words mean 'Edward VII [the king at this time], by the Grace of God, King of all British people, Defender of the Faith, Emperor of India'*

Study **Source A**. How useful is **Source A** to a historian studying the British Empire in the early twentieth century? Explain your answer using **Source A** and your contextual knowledge.

8 marks

Revision progress

Sample student answer

Source A is useful to a historian studying the British Empire in the early twentieth century as it shows how big the British Empire was. The map shows that the empire spread across the globe. It also shows that the empire was built around trade, as all the colonies can be reached by sea. Some people are critical of the British Empire as it exploited countries such as India and took their raw materials. This was also the case with African nations that were in the empire, such as South Africa which lay in the trade route with India. The British took raw materials such as rubber, timber and coffee. The goods would be taken from the colonies to Britain where they would be sold to other British colonies – so the British made all of the money from it. A historian studying the British Empire would find this source useful as it shows the way that the British took over lands that were by the sea so they could easily remove and profit from their raw materials. The source is also useful to a historian studying the British Empire as it shows how proud Britain was of its empire, and how Britain saw itself as the leading country of the empire, just as the lion is often referred to as a 'king' in the animal kingdom. This source shows Britain's dominance.

EXAMINER TIP

Try not to write only about what you can see in the picture but also about what facts you know. For example, the British taking raw materials from the colonies is a key feature of the empire.

EXAMINER TIP

The question asks about 'how useful' the source is and this answer directly refers to the reason the British Empire is mostly coastal. The answer shows that the British used the colonies to make money.

OVERALL COMMENT

The answer is a good answer at Level 3 because it uses what can be seen in the picture and adds some extra knowledge. To secure a Level 3 it would need to add another point from the source and discuss provenance. Another point, for example, could be about the lion surrounded by the animals of the empire and what this tells us about British authority in the empire.

OVER TO YOU

1 Review the sample answer:
   a highlight where the answer adds some factual knowledge
   b highlight where the answer uses the provenance (caption information).

2 a Now have a go at writing your own answer. Remember, in the exam it is recommended that you spend no more than 10 minutes on this question.
   b Once you have written your answer, check it against the questions below. Did you…
   ☐ include some detailed facts and figures?
   ☐ remember to refer to the provenance of the source?
   ☐ make your answer relevant to what the historian is studying?

You may find it helpful to look back at Chapters 7 and 8 to refresh your knowledge of the growth of the British Empire.

EXAMINER TIP

Activities **1a** and **b** will help you build your own answer. Remember to always start by describing what you can see in the source, then identify what this tells you about the question being asked, and then finally add in your own knowledge.

Exam practice

The 'significance' question

> **EXAM QUESTION:** Explain the significance of Sir Walter Raleigh for the British Empire.
>
> 8 marks

Sample student answer

Sir Walter Raleigh is significant because he set up the first British colony in North America. This was the colony of Roanoke, and he set it up in 1584 for Queen Elizabeth I. The colony was not a success; it was plagued by disease, and indigenous American tribes living there carried out massacres. However, Raleigh showed that it was possible to start a colony in North America. This was especially important when the next monarch, James I, wanted to start a colony, as he sent Raleigh to do that. Raleigh set up the colony of Jamestown in Virginia. This colony showed the profit that could be made from growing tobacco; this would go on to be one of the main commodities of the British Empire, showing another reason why Raleigh is significant for the British Empire.

Raleigh is also significant because he influenced other colonists. His first settlement in North America led to other settlements being established, until Britain controlled the east coast of America as part of its empire. America was an important part of the British Empire and brought a lot of money and power to Britain. This is why Raleigh is remembered as the 'Father of American Colonies'.

EXAMINER TIP
This answer shows a range of accurate knowledge and understanding that is relevant to the question.

EXAMINER TIP
The answer explains two aspects of significance. Firstly, how Raleigh established tobacco as a crop and secondly, how his colony led to British control in America.

OVERALL COMMENT

The answer is largely a Level 3 response. It gives two developed points of significance. To push beyond a Level 3 it would need to show how the significance of Raleigh changed over time.

OVER TO YOU

1. Review the sample answer:
   a. highlight the technical terms used in the answer
   b. highlight where the answer mentions the impact of Walter Raleigh.

2. a. Now have a go at writing your own answer. Remember, in the exam it is recommended that you spend no more than 10 minutes on this question.
   b. Once you have written your answer, check it against the questions below. Did you…
      - [ ] include some detailed knowledge?
      - [ ] remember to provide at least two examples of the significance of Walter Raleigh?

You may find it helpful to look back at Chapter 5 to refresh your knowledge of Raleigh and British expansion in North America.

Revision progress

The 'similarity' question

EXAM QUESTION: Explain two ways in which the expansion of the British Empire in India and the expansion of the British Empire in Africa were similar.

8 marks

Sample student answer

The expansion of the British Empire in India and the expansion of the British Empire in Africa were similar because of the reactions to the expansion. Both the Indian people and those in African nations controlled by Britain staged uprisings against the British expansion. The Sepoys in India rebelled in 1857 when the British expansion meant that British customs were being forced upon Muslim Sepoys. There was a feeling that the British did not care about the Indians and their culture and customs. The rebellion was put down brutally by British forces. This was similar to the African rebellions against British expansion as land and resources were taken away from the Africans, for example under Cecil Rhodes in the Transvaal. There was a feeling that traditional life was destroyed by British expansion.

Both examples of expansion are also similar because of the reasons for expansion. Both India and Africa offered raw materials that could be exploited by the British. The commodities would be taken from the colonies and then sold to other countries in the empire – this made Britain a lot of money. Another reason the British expanded into India and Africa was for religious reasons. Christian missionaries felt it was their duty to bring Christianity to the colonies. This removed existing religious traditions.

EXAMINER TIP

This answer is good because it immediately identifies a similarity.

EXAMINER TIP

This answer could have reached Level 4 if it had provided details about similarities in, for example, beliefs and attitudes, in the two time periods. At both the time of expansion in India and expansion in Africa, there was a belief that Britain had a right to take the land, and that the white British were superior.

OVERALL COMMENT

The answer is a Level 3. It shows some detailed knowledge but might be improved by adding more detail or explanation about the similarities in the conflicts between the British and those taking part in uprisings in Africa and India.

OVER TO YOU

1. Review the sample answer:
   a. highlight where the answer shows it is concerned with similarity
   b. highlight where the answer shows relevant knowledge
   c. highlight where the answer adds knowledge that is not directly related to the question.

2. a. Now have a go at writing your own answer. Remember, in the exam it is recommended that you spend no more than 10 minutes on this question.
   b. Once you have written your answer, check it against the questions below. Did you…
      ☐ suggest at least two similarities?
      ☐ make sure that they share a common theme or point?
      ☐ include some detailed facts from your own knowledge to support each similarity?

You may find it helpful to look back at Chapters 7 and 8 to refresh your knowledge of the expansion of the British Empire in India and the expansion of the British Empire in Africa.

Britain: Migration, Empires and the People c790–Present Day

Exam practice

The 'main factors' question

> **EXAM QUESTION:** Has economic resources been the main factor in causing migration to Britain since Medieval times? Explain your answer with reference to economic resources and other factors.
>
> **16 marks** **SPaG 4 marks**

Sample student answer

Economic resources are the most important factor in causing migration to Britain from Medieval times to the present day. The Viking invasions in the Medieval period were caused by a desire to make money and build a strong empire. This caused more migration with the creation of Danelaw and then the consolidation of power under Cnut and Emma of Normandy and their North Sea Empire. The nineteenth century saw increased migration to Britain because of economic resources; for example many people came from Ireland to work as navvies, building the canals that were emerging during the Industrial Revolution. Hundreds of thousands more Irish people arrived in Britain in the 1840s because of the potato famine of 1846, which killed over a million people and left others starving and in need of food and work. Similarly, the twentieth century saw further migration to Britain because of economic resources as the British Nationality Act of 1948 stated that British passport holders could come to Britain to work. This led to people from Commonwealth countries, like Jamaica, to come and work in the new NHS and other industries.

Although economic resources are the most important factor, another important factor in causing migration to Britain that also feeds economic resources has been religion. Religious persecution has caused groups to seek refuge in Britain to worship in freedom. The Huguenots of France came to Britain in the sixteenth century to escape persecution by French Catholics. Under Elizabeth I England was a Protestant country and so the Huguenots were able to come and worship and live in peace. In the nineteenth century Jewish migration to Britain was caused by persecution in Russia. Jews were blamed for the assassination of the Tsar and so they faced restrictions and pogroms. Coming to Britain was a way to escape this persecution.

EXAMINER TIP: This answer is good as it gives examples of migration from many different time periods.

EXAMINER TIP: This point should be developed to show how economic resources and religion influence each other. The answer should show how various factors influence each other.

OVERALL COMMENT

The answer is good because it gives examples of economic factors from across the whole time period covered by the unit. It is a strong Level 3 because it has explained how economic factors as well as religion caused migration to Britain. There is good spelling and grammar in the answer and it uses the correct historical terms. However, to be sure of a Level 3 it would benefit from another factor. For Level 4 the judgement about economic resources being the most important factor should be developed and compared to another factor.

OVER TO YOU

1. Review the sample answer. Highlight where the following are mentioned:

   a economic resources as a factor in causing migration to Britain

   b other factors

   c how each factor acted to cause migration.

2. Now have a go at writing your own answer. Remember, in the exam it is recommended that you spend no more than 20 minutes on this question.

   a Write a paragraph about another factor related to the causes of migration to Britain.

   b Write a conclusion in which you compare the influence of the main factor with another factor.

   c Once you have written your answer, check it against the questions below. Did you…

   ☐ write about a factor other than the one mentioned in the question?

   ☐ add some factual knowledge of your own?

   ☐ make a decision about which factor was the main factor?

   ☐ check your answer for correct spellings, punctuation and grammar?

> **EXAMINER TIP**
>
> You have only 20 minutes to answer this question so a paragraph should take about 5 minutes.

> **EXAMINER TIP**
>
> When planning your response to this question try to show how factors link together. This will help you explain 'relative impact' in your response.

Activity answers guidance

The answers provided here are examples, based on the information provided in the Recap sections of this Revision Guide. There may be other factors which are relevant to each question, and you should draw on as much of your own knowledge as possible to give detailed and precise answers. There are also many ways of answering exam questions (for example, of structuring an essay). However, these exemplar answers should provide a good starting point.

Chapter 1
Page 13
SOURCE ANALYSIS

a   Your answer should include the following: Battle of Edington, protecting Wessex, bringing peace, creating Danelaw.

b   You may pick any of the events that show control, e.g. the creation of Danelaw showed Alfred had more control. This brought in a period of peace.

c   Your graph should show that initially the Vikings were dominant, and then through Alfred's military victory and his peace talks and negotiating, the Anglo-Saxons had more control.

d   Source A is useful to a historian studying Viking challenges to Anglo-Saxon control as it shows the invading force heading to Lindisfarne. This was a tactic used by the Vikings – they would attack coastal towns to raid them and weaken Anglo-Saxon control. Vikings invaded these areas because they knew that Britain had resources and land, something that was lacking in Scandinavia. Vikings would set up settlements once they had control of areas inland. This would weaken Anglo-Saxon control and would eventually lead to the creation of Danelaw, a Viking controlled area of England.

Page 15
FACTORS

a   Your answer should include the actions the Vikings took when attempting to conquer Britain:
   - using their fleet to invade
   - rebellions
   - battles.

b   Your spider diagram should include:
   Anglo-Saxon: 1002 Aethelred – mass killing of Vikings; Aethelred pushed Cnut back to Denmark
   Viking: 991 Sven Forkbeard and Olaf Tryggvason, Battle of Maldon; 1013 Sven Forkbeard invasion; 1014–16 Viking rebellion in England; October 1016 Cnut won Battle of Assandun giving Cnut control of everywhere apart from Wessex

c   Your answer could include:
   - Marriage to Aethelred formed alliance with Normandy to help reduce Viking raids
   - Married Cnut, bringing more lands to the North Sea Empire
   - Strong leader in Cnut's absence
   - Improved relations with the the Church

d   Your answer should include an analysis of war as the main factor, and at least one other factor, before having a conclusion, for example:

War: this was undoubtedly a factor leading to the North Sea Empire. Although much of Cnut's land was inherited, he secured control of Britain by fighting battles such as the Battle of Assandun which gave him control of all of England apart from Wessex. However, when Edmund died in 1016 Cnut controlled Britain which made his North Sea Empire stronger as Britain made him lots of money.

Role of the individual: this was also a factor which led to Cnut's North Sea Empire. Cnut inherited lots of land through birth, marriage and battle and this created the North Sea Empire. However, another individual who is important for the consolidation of this empire was Emma of Normandy. Not only did she own land that then became part of the North Sea Empire, but she was also a strong leader who was respected and listened to, she was good with money and brought peace to England. It is fair to argue that without her leadership the North Sea Empire would not have been as successful.

Conclusion: although Cnut secured his empire through battles and wars it remained strong and successful because of the role of the individual. Without Cnut and Emma of Normandy managing war and peace the empire would not have been as much of a success.

Chapter 2
Page 17
SIMILARITY

a   Your answer might include:
   French became the language of those in power / Churches, cathedrals and monasteries were built/ Land was taken away and given to the Normans/ England was looked after by William of Normandy's barons and lords

b   Land was taken away and given to the Normans; England was looked after by William of Normandy's barons and lords; his sons took over when he died

c   The invasion of Sven Forkbeard in 1013 and the Norman invasion of 1066 are similar when considering the causes. Both forces invaded England with the view of making it part of their empire and taking control of the country. Both forces were confident that they should have control of England. Forkbeard was trying to claim back land that had been taken from Vikings in the tenth century. William of Normandy argued that King Edward and Harold Godwinson had agreed that he should take the throne.

Another similarity is the methods used by both Sven Forkbeard and William of Normandy. They both used a fleet and then an army to invade and try to secure control of England. In both 991 and 1014 Forkbeard invaded England and fought the English. In 1066 William of Normandy invaded and fought the English at Hastings. Both forces were successful against the English.

Page 19
FACTORS

a   Your table might include, for example:
   Event/individuals/factor
   - Richard I spent a long period of his reign in France or on crusades, losing land in France/Phillip II and Richard II/role of the individual; war
   - King John became king and lost land in France/John I and Richard/role of the individual
   - Phillip II conquered Normandy, Anjou, Maine and Brittany/Phillip II/role of the individual; war

b   Your mind-map should include:
   War: Richard I fighting crusades and not protecting lands in France; English regions facing invasions from Phillip II; King John is bad in battle and loses Brittany, Normandy, Anjou and Maine (he is so bad in battle he is known as 'softsword')
   Role of the individual: Phillip II of France – invading Normandy and Anjou; King John being such a poor leader that he could not control his barons and was forced to sign Magna Carta

c   Your answer should include an analysis of war as the main factor, and at least one other factor, for example:

War: an important factor in the collapse of the Angevin Empire because it was lost battles that led to the land being taken away. For example, when Phillip II of France captured Normandy and Anjou, this was the start of the vast Angevin Empire that had been inherited through birth and marriage being lost. Furthermore, under King John, the English army were no match for the French. The English were so unsuccessful that John got the nickname 'softsword'. However, not all of the blame can be given to John as his brother before him, Richard I, did not focus on protecting the Angevin Empire and so lost key territories. This shows why war is an important factor in causing the end of the Angevin Empire.

Role of the individual: the most important factor for the collapse of the Angevin Empire was the role of the individual. King John

66   Activity answers guidance

was not just bad in battle, he was not good at keeping the peace in England. His poor leadership lost the remaining territory in France. John did not listen to the English barons; they were angry about increased taxes. The barons made John sign Magna Carta to respect the rights of the barons. John's poor leadership and poor battle record meant that the Angevin Empire went from controlling large areas in France to control of Gascony only.

Chapter 3
Page 21
EXPLAIN THE SIGNIFICANCE

a England became very rich, and developed its empire.

b England: gains English identity; France: becomes unified under one king

c The ideas of national identity that emerged after the Hundred Years War can still be seen today as France is still a unified country. It was after the Hundred Years War that it united as one state. Similarly, in England the Hundred Years War saw a move away from its links with France. The country was seen as apart from Europe and there was a move away from using French words. This is still the case today and even more so since Britain left the European Union in 2020.

d The Hundred Years War was significant for English identity because at the time it allowed England to move away from French influences and create a common language and homeland. Previously, people had identified more with the region they were from, whereas after the Hundred Years War they saw themselves as English. This shows the Hundred Years War was significant for the English identity because it had an impact on culture.

Another way in which the Hundred Years War was significant is that the new English identity allowed England, and then Britain, to look at conquering lands outside of Europe. The move away from France meant that England wanted to find new lands to take over. This was significant for the English identity because the empire became a big part of England's history.

We can still see the significance of the Hundred Years War today when we consider the language we use. After the Hundred Years War there was a move away from French being the national language and a focus on English instead; this is still the case today.

Chapter 4
Page 23
FACTORS

a You might make a flashcard for each cause but it would be wise to categorise them into factors. Your flashcards may look like this:

Economic: new land for new cash crops (plantations)

Religious: Puritans and Catholics escaping religious conflict and persecution

Imperialist ideas: the plantations helped the growth of the British Empire

b A push factor is something that would make people leave their homes in Europe and a pull factor would be something good about America that would make them want to go.

c Your answer must explain how economic resources were a factor in Tudor and Stuart ambitions (as the named factor), plus at least one other factor of your choice. You should include reference to the plantation system, cash crops and privateering. Another factor could be imperialist ideas as America became an extension of England's empire – specific reference to John Hawkins and Walter Raleigh would develop these points well.

Page 25
EXPLAIN THE SIGNIFICANCE

a
- Enslaved people were cheaper
- Plantation owners could buy enslaved people outright
- Enslaved people had no legal rights
- Any children born to enslaved people became their owner's property

b Traders would leave Britain with ships full of goods headed for Africa. These goods would be traded with African tribesman for prisoners from other African tribes. These enslaved Africans would be taken to America where they would be traded for sugar, cotton or tobacco to be taken back to Britain.

c Your mind-map might include:
- Created profits
- Created jobs
- Coastal cities grew
- Encouraged imperialist ideas

d Your answer should explain the relationship between aspects of significance, for example over time, supported by factual knowledge and understanding. It is vital to explain short-term and long-term impacts of the slave trade on the expansion of the British Empire.

Chapter 5
Page 27
SIMILARITY

a
- Converting indigenous Americans to Christianity
- Moved the indigenous Americans out of their territory
- Forcing European culture on indigenous Americans

b Profiles could be made on the following:
- Puritans
- James I
- Walter Raleigh

Remember to give key dates, statistics and events.

c When constructing your paragraph you should consider the following:
- The settlers brought diseases
- The lack of respect
- The natives were moved off their land
- The indigenous American way of life was wiped out

When making your judgement you should give a clear opinion at the start of the paragraph and refer to it throughout.

d Your answer should cover two points of comparison – for example, detailed references to motivations for colonising America and detailed references to the success and legacy of each colony.

Page 29
SOURCE ANALYSIS

a & b **Political reasons:** lack of respect for the aristocratic rule of Britain, lack of representations

Economic reasons: taxation, Navigation Acts, Stamp Act, monopoly

c Taxation angered the colonists because it was used to pay for British wars with the French and the colonists felt it had very little to do with them. Furthermore, the colonists had a strong economy which they felt was separate from Britain's, so why should the money go to Britain?

d Your answer will draw on your contextual knowledge to question critically the content and provenance of the source. You should reference its usefulness in relation to showing the economic causes of the War of Independence, with the painting depicting the Boston Tea Party. This would lead to a wider explanation of taxation and economic independence being a cause of the war.

Chapter 6
Page 31
SOURCE ANALYSIS

a
- Religious civil wars between the 1560s and 1590s
- St Bartholomew's Day Massacre
- Elizabeth I's Protestantism made England safe for Huguenots
- King Louis XIV made being Protestant heresy

b
- Established businesses
- Developed new industries such as papermaking
- Contributed to business, art and craft

c
- Women weaving
- Using a spinning wheel
- Working hard
- Old and young working together

d Your answer should point out that the source is useful to show the work Huguenots did and the contribution they made to society. You could reference the information in activity b.

Chapter 7
Page 33
SIMILARITY

a Your answer might include:
- India was rich in natural resources (iron ore, silk, copper, gold, silver) – so any country that made strong trade links with India might get access to these goods
- India was an important base for much of Britain's growing global trading
- India was an important colonial possession after Britain lost the valuable American colonies in the late 1700s
- India was a good place in which to sell goods to the many millions of Indians

b Wars broke out across India and the Mughals began to lose control of the country. Some European nations took advantage of this and began to expand their control over India. Dutch, French and British companies, including the EIC, supported particular Indian princes with weapons and soldiers in return for rewards such as land or goods.

c Your answer might include:
- Set up in 1600; monopoly over British trade in India
- EIC traded British goods in countries as far away as Japan
- Fine china, silk, coffee and spices brought back to Britain
- In 1700s, the EIC began to take more and more Indian land
- It used its private army and navy against regional rulers of India

d Your answer will use the information on the pages to create a timeline. This might start with, for example:
- In the 1500s, the Mughals invade India and take control of areas mostly run by Hindu princes

e Your answer might include detail on the following:
- Conflict played a major part in the expansion. You could then expand on the conflicts in America with indigenous tribes and the conflicts in India with both other European nations and local princes (such as at the Battle of Plassey)
- Economic factors were a major reason behind the expansion – both areas were rich in natural resources. You could give examples of those resources

Page 35
SOURCE ANALYSIS

a Your answer will outline the causes of the Indian Rebellion using the information on the pages. They might include, for example:
- The British ignored or replaced long-standing Indian traditions, rights and customs
- They also replaced the Indian aristocracy; this led to widespread frustration and discontentment

b Your answer might focus on the different perspectives of different nations. Indians saw this as the first chapter in the struggle for independence, while the British saw it as a rebellion against their rule.

c There was a massacre of 200 British women and children.

d It outraged the British, and crowds cried for blood. Soon after, Queen Victoria sent 70,000 fresh troops to India.

e You might describe the woman, representing Britain (Britannia) taking revenge on the local population. The caption reads 'Justice'.

f Your answer should reflect an evaluation of the source with a sustained judgement based on content and provenance. You should reference the fact that it is a British source that justifies the response to the massacre at Cawnpore.

Page 37
EXPLAIN THE SIGNIFICANCE

a Your quiz will reflect the content of the spread.

b Your answer will reflect that some people saw India benefitting in some way from British rule (the British had built thousands of kilometres of roads, as well as many schools, hospitals, factories and railways) while others think India was exploited (British customs were forced on the people and local traditions, culture and religions tended to be ignored).

c Your answer should explain the relationship between aspects of significance, for example over time, supported by factual knowledge and understanding. It is vital to explain the short-term and long-term impact of British control both in India and Britain.

Chapter 8
Page 39
SIMILARITY

a Your answer might include: Africa was rich in natural resources; the Europeans could sell their goods to the people who lived there; some felt it was their duty to convert people to Christianity and travelled through Africa preaching about Christianity; some European countries simply competed to build large empires.

b Your answer might include, for example:

Political factors: some European countries competed to build large empires; between 1880 and 1900, there was a race to grab as much of Africa as possible before another country got there first. This led to the Berlin Conference of 1884

Economic factors: Africa was rich in natural resources – gold, diamonds and ivory, as well as 'cash crops' such as rubber, coffee and timber. Some countries looked to Africa as a way of getting even richer, and if European countries controlled huge areas of Africa, they could sell their goods to the people who lived there

c Your answer will cover two points of comparison – for example, economic factors played a key role in expansion in both areas. Also, there was a degree of resistance in each area from the people who lived there.

Page 41
SOURCE ANALYSIS

a It was an important trade link between the Mediterranean Sea and the Indian Ocean; a vital route for Britain's access to India (80 per cent of ships using the canal were British); and it reduced the journey time from London to Mumbai by two weeks.

b Your answer will reflect the detail in the timeline on page 40.

c Your answer will draw on your contextual knowledge to question critically the content and provenance of the source. You should reference its usefulness in relation to showing the importance of the canal as a gateway to India – represented by a key – with Disraeli and the Great Sphinx exchanging a smirk and a knowing glance because they know the importance of the purchase.

Page 43
FACTORS

a Your cards should reflect the key information in relation to the headings given.

b Your answer must explain how economic resources were a factor in British involvement (as the named factor), plus at least one other factor of your choice. The example in the tip might encourage you to write that ideas about imperialism and social Darwinism led the British to believe they were racially superior and had a 'right' to the land they conquered. Also, ideas and jingoism in relation to the empire were spread to keep the public's opinion of it high and to win their support when taking over more land abroad.

Chapter 9
Page 45
EXPLAIN THE SIGNIFICANCE

a i) When migrants move because they choose to leave a particular place of their own free will, rather than being forced to
   ii) When migrants move because they have no choice and are forced to

b Your answer is your opinion, but it should be justified with a reason. For example, you might write that Irish migration was mixed – some were forced to leave as a result of poverty/famine while others came looking for job opportunities.

c Your answer might reflect the problems highlighted in the spread. For example, Jewish people faced anger and hostility towards them, mainly because they were accused of taking jobs from British workers. A campaign to stop Jewish immigration began in the late 1800s, supported by key politicians. In 1905, the number of Jewish immigrants was limited.

d   Your answer should explain the relationship between aspects of significance, for example over time, supported by factual knowledge and understanding. It is vital to explain short term and long term impacts of Irish migration into Britain.

Page 47
SIMILARITY

a   Your definitions will be based on your understanding of the terms, for example, 'urbanisation is when large numbers of people move to towns and cities from rural areas'.

b   Your answer should give details about the two main causes – migration from abroad and rural to urban migration.

c   Your answer should cover two points of comparison – for example, detailed references to forced migration as well as detailed references to the voluntary migration that also took place.

Chapter 10
Page 49
FACTORS

a   Your answer might include that Africans and Indians had fought for freedom for Britain in the war, and so felt their own countries should be free.

b   Your revision cards will reflect the information given in the spread.

c   You should show a range of accurate and detailed knowledge and understanding in your answer. You should write how the factor of war(s) was key, and how it contributed to Indian independence – and also look at another factor(s) such as the role of individuals.

Page 51
SIMILARITY

a   Your revision cards should reflect the information given in the spread.

b   Your answer might include:
    Similarities: strong independence movements; violence often flared up; often focused around one dominant leader; often saw large movements of people during the process; official groups often associated with the independence movements
    Differences: British reaction more extreme/violent in some places than others; not all independence leaders were jailed

c   Your answer might focus on: strong independence movements in each colony; violence often flared up; often focused around one dominant leader; often saw large movements of people during the process; official groups often associated with the independence movements.

Chapter 11
Page 53
SOURCE ANALYSIS

a   The cartoon shows a black family, looking fed up, outside a house with a sign that says 'No Entry'. They have all their luggage with them showing they have not found anywhere to settle.

b   The message is that black immigrants were finding it hard to find accommodation and were not able to settle in Britain. The caption also lets us know that the Commonwealth was not seen as a good thing by everyone at this point.

c   By 1961 a lot of people from the Caribbean and Asia had arrived in Britain. Anti-immigrant feeling had increased and clashes had started between white and non-white communities. There were issues around housing and employment for the immigrants, and segregation.

d   Anti-immigrant feeling had become such a problem that the new Commonwealth Immigrant Acts were being passed through parliament (first act passed in 1962). They were designed to limit the amount of immigration from Commonwealth countries to the UK. The series of reforms that followed showed that the British government wanted to change immigration and many people saw these changes as being against black people.

e   You can use your answers to parts **a** to **d** to answer this question. You may want to add that the source is useful because the cartoonist worked for the Evening Standard, a London newspaper. This shows that government responses to immigration were important and were having an impact on society.

Page 55
SOURCE ANALYSIS

a   Your answer might include:
    • Poverty and hardship were common. Jamaica had been devastated by a hurricane in 1944. The tourist industry had not yet developed to provide jobs
    • Many West Indians had been taught in school that Britain was a 'mother country'. Britain was short of workers so people were encouraged to move there. It was seen as a great opportunity – they felt very 'British' and had been educated to love Britain
    • In 1948, the British Nationality Act was passed. All who lived within the British Empire – the Commonwealth – were British passport holders and were entitled to live and work in Britain

b   It was a ship that brought the first of many migrants from the Caribbean (known as the West Indies) to the UK.

c   Your answer should point out that the source is useful to show the strength of feeling by some against migration. You might reference the information in the flow diagram on page 54.

Page 57
SOURCE ANALYSIS

a   They are in the southern Atlantic Ocean, off the east coast of Argentina.

b   Your answer will include, for example: Argentina felt the islands were rightfully theirs because Britain seized the uninhabited islands from Argentina in 1833, and British settlers began to live there. Another reason might be that the Argentinian economy was having severe problems in the early 1980s and Galtieri (the Argentinian leader) hoped that a successful war (ending with the return of the Falklands) would restore national morale and belief in his government.

c   You might list the seizure of the islands in 1833 as a long-term reason and the attempt by Galtieri to restore national pride as a short-term reason.

d   You should write down a short-, medium- and long-term impact in your own words.

e   Your answer should point out that the source is useful for showing a positive response by the British public in Liverpool to the Falklands War and a possible increase in patriotic feeling in the country. You might also reference the content on page 57 about the war's impact on Thatcher's popularity and point out that Liverpool was not pro-Thatcher yet the population there still got behind the war.

Chapter 12
Page 59
FACTORS

a   Your list might include opportunities such as work and education, but also reasons such as escaping poverty, war and persecution.

b   You should explain the stated factor (in this case, war) and other factor(s). Your answer should demonstrate a range of accurate knowledge and understanding that is relevant to the question. For example, you may reference the Second World War as a reason why many Poles fled to Britain. In recent years, a growing number of refugees have come into the EU from war-torn countries like Afghanistan, Iraq and Syria. However, you should also reference at least one other factor, for example, economic factors. For example, this was the cause of much of the Irish migration, and many generations had come before 1945. Further groups migrating in the 1950s and 1960s came to join families or look for work, and to escape poverty and hardship in Ireland.

Britain: Migration, Empires and the People c790–Present Day

Glossary

asylum protection given by a country to someone who has left their home country

baron man who had been given high rank by the king; the title came with land

Catholic Christian who who follows the teachings of the Catholic Church

civil war war between different groups in one country

commodity goods that are traded for other goods; this might be food, produce or even enslaved people

Commonwealth voluntary association of independent nations and dependent territories linked by historical ties (as parts of the former British Empire) and cooperating on matters of mutual concern, especially regarding economics and trade

crusade religious war fought in the Middle Ages between Christians and Muslims

Danegeld land tax levied in Anglo-Saxon England to raise funds for protection against Danish invaders

Danelaw part of northern and eastern England occupied and controlled by Danes from the late ninth century until after the Norman Conquest

diaspora group of people from a small geographical area scattered across different countries

dominion semi-independent country that was part of the British Empire but had its own government

Edict of Nantes agreement granting Protestants civil rights in France in 1598; revoked in 1685 by Louis XIV of France

empire collection of tribes, regions, territories, states or countries that are ruled over and controlled by one leader or 'mother country'; the areas controlled are usually called colonies (although sometimes dominions or dependencies); the mother country makes many of the key decisions to do with the places it rules over

enslaved made a slave; having one's freedom to choose or act taken away

exclusion zone area into which entry is forbidden, especially by ships or aircraft from particular nations

forced migration when migrants move because they have no choice and are forced to

guerrilla member of small group of soldiers who do not belong to a regular army; they usually fight as independent units and wage small-scale attacks on their enemies

heretic non-believer, or believer in an opposing religion

Highland Clearances forced eviction during the eighteenth and nineteenth centuries of a large number of people from land they farmed in the Scottish Highlands

imperial propaganda a government's attempts to spread a set of ideas and beliefs about empire and conquest

imperialist person who practises/supports imperialism, which is a set of ideas and beliefs about empire and conquest

indenture system migrants would agree to work for a period of five years in return for a basic wage and transport to their new workplace. The worker was to be returned at the end of the period of service to the port of departure. Some came home when the work was done, but thousands stayed

indentured servant servant who paid for their passage to a new country by signing a contract stating that they would work for a certain number of years for their master

indigenous originating from a particular place; native

internal migration refers to people within a country moving to another location within its borders

Jacobite Rebellions rebellions in the 1700s that aimed to help the Stuarts regain the British throne; 'Jacobus' is Latin for James, the first Stuart king of England

jingoism feeling or belief that a person's country is always right; in favour of aggressive acts against other countries

Magna Carta document written in 1215 that recognised people's rights to certain basic liberties

Mau Mau Rebellion military conflict that took place in British Kenya, between 1952 and 1960, between groups that wanted Kenya to become an independent nation and British forces who wished Kenya to remain part of the British Empire

monopoly complete control of the entire supply of goods or of a service in a certain area

nationalism having strong patriotic feelings, especially a belief in the superiority of one's own country over others

navvy labourer employed in building a road or railway

net migration final change in population after all the people leaving a country (emigrating) and all the people moving into a country (immigrating) have been taken into account

plantation large farm that specialises in growing usually just one crop

plunder to steal from a place or person, usually using force

pogrom large-scale, targeted, an repeated persecution of an ethnic or religious group, particularly Jews

Puritan hard-line Protestant Christian who believes in simple church services and lifestyles; Puritans protested against the practices of the Catholic Church

Quaker member of a Protestant Christian group also known as the Religious Society of Friends, that believes in equality between members

scorched earth military strategy that involves destroying anything that might be useful to the enemy while advancing through or withdrawing from an area

sepoy native Indian soldier

single market shared agreement that means that goods, services, money and people can move freely between EU member countries

slave triangle three-part trading journey in which traders traded goods for enslaved Africans (slaves); enslaved people for different goods in the Americas; and these goods for money in Britain

social Darwinism based on Darwin's theory of evolution, which said that weaker animals would die out and stronger ones would evolve and survive. This was applied to countries or peoples. Darwin's theory made people like Cecil Rhodes think it was right for those they perceived as stronger (and therefore 'superior') like Britain to take over weaker countries

Stamp Act act that imposed a tax on printed materials (such as legal documents, magazines, playing cards and newspapers) paid to Britain and used in the colonies of British America

trading station large warehouse at a port where goods were stored and where trading took place

tribe a social group made up of families or communities linked by social, economic, or religious similarities, often with a common culture and language.

urbanisation process by which large numbers of people move to urban areas, creating larger towns and cities

viceroy someone who rules in another country or colony on behalf of the monarch

Viking Scandinavian pirates and traders who raided and settled in many parts of northern Europe in the eighth to the eleventh centuries

voluntary migration when migrants move because they choose to leave a particular place of their own free will, rather than being forced to

Witan national council or parliament in Anglo-Saxon England

Topics available from Oxford AQA GCSE History

Germany 1890–1945: Democracy and Dictatorship
Student Book
978 019 837010 9
Kerboodle Book
978 019 837014 7

America 1920–1973: Opportunity and Inequality
Student Book
978 019 841262 5
Kerboodle Book
978 019 841263 2

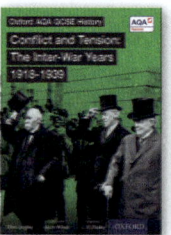

Conflict and Tension: The Inter-War Years 1918–1939
Student Book
978 019 837011 6
Kerboodle Book
978 019 837015 4

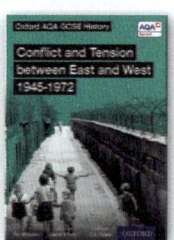

Conflict and Tension between East and West 1945–1972
Student Book
978 019 841266 3
Kerboodle Book
978 019 841267 0

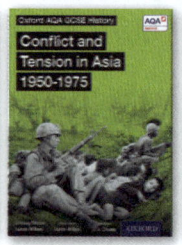

Conflict and Tension in Asia 1950–1975
Student Book
978 019 841264 9
Kerboodle Book
978 019 841265 6

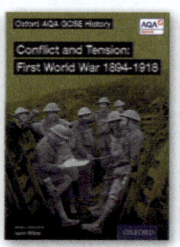

Conflict and Tension First World War 1894-1918
Student Book
978 019 842900 5
Kerboodle Book
978 019 842901 2

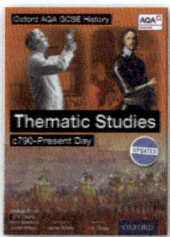

Thematic Studies c790–Present Day
Student Book
978 019 837013 0
Kerboodle Book
978 019 837017 8

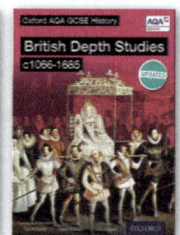

British Depth Studies c1066–1685
Student Book
978 019 837012 3
Kerboodle Book
978 019 837016 1

RECAP • APPLY • REVIEW • SUCCEED

Germany 1890–1945 Revision Guide
978 019 842289 1

America 1920–1973: Opportunity and Inequality Revision Guide
978 019 843282 1

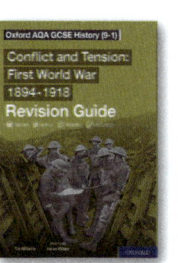

Conflict and Tension First World War 1894–1918 Revision Guide
978 138 200767 2

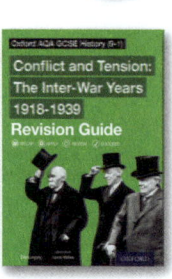

Conflict and Tension: The Inter-War Years 1918–1939 Revision Guide
978 019 842291 4

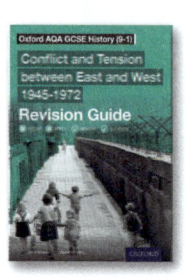

Conflict and Tension between East and West 1945–1972 Revision Guide
978 019 843288 3

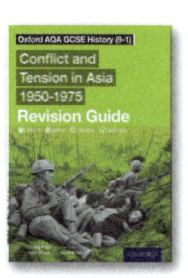

Conflict and Tension in Asia 1950–1975 Revision Guide
978 019 843286 9

Britain: Health and the People c1000–Present Day Revision Guide
978 019 842295 2

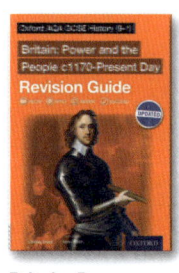

Britain: Power and the People c1170–Present Day Revision Guide
978 019 843290 6

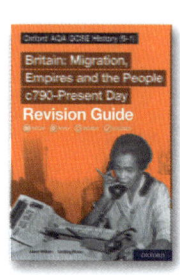

Britain: Migration, Empires and the People c790-Present Day Revision Guide
978 138 201503 5

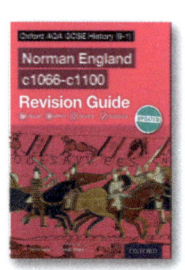

Norman England c1066–c.1100 Revision Guide
978 019 843284 5

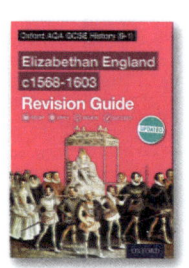

Elizabethan England c1568–1603 Revision Guide
978 019 842293 8

Time-saving expert support for all 16 AQA options

Teacher Handbook
978 019 837018 5
Professional, practical support filled with subject knowledge, classroom ideas and activities, plus exam advice and support.

Kerboodle Exam Practice and Revision
978 019 037019 2
An online resource packed full of exam practice, revision and continuing timesaving support for the entire specification.

All published Student Books have been approved by AQA. The Kerboodle: Exam Practice and Revision, Teacher Handbook, and Revision Guides have not been approved by AQA.

Order online at **www.oxfordsecondary.com/gcsehistory**